I0520995

Everything I Needed to Survive in Life

I Learned from the U.S. Army

FM 18-66

C.S. Stahlman

Copyright © 2025 C.S. Stahlman.

All rights reserved. No part of this publication may be reproduced, stored in a retrieval system, or transmitted in any form or by any means—electronic, mechanical, photocopy, recording, or any other—except for brief quotations in printed reviews, without the prior written permission of the author.

ISBN: 979-8-9992218-0-3

Published in the United States of America

Contents

FOREWORD

C.S. Stahlman and I first met in 1976 when we were both students at Westminster College in Fulton, MO. He was a freshman, and I was a junior. We played on the Independent Student Association intramural sports teams and had the shared experience of being enrolled in the Army Reserve Officer Training Corps program. I knew him mostly by his last name (as ROTC Cadets are inclined) and then by his middle name, Scott.

Scott and I had several differences. He was commissioned into the Signal Corps branch, which focuses on Information Technology. I was commissioned into the Field Artillery branch, one of our Army's combat branches. Scott spent seven years on Active Duty, and I spent thirty-three. I experienced multiple combat deployments; he had none.

One can focus on the differences between Scott and me. But there are two things that bind us that no one can challenge. First, both of us took an oath of office as commissioned officers. That oath is a bedrock of allegiance to the U.S. Constitution. The oath connects us to others who serve or have served by establishing a shared, solemn commitment to the same constitutional principles. The other is a commonality between veterans which includes service to country, shared values such as honor, resilience, and commitment to sacrifice and dedication.

The lessons Scott documents convince me that, beyond maintaining readiness to protect our national interests, a military career of any duration benefits not only the nation but also provides a tremendous opportunity for growth to inculcate a spirit of selflessness, loyalty, accountability, and compassion.

I also fully endorse his recommendations on providing care to our veterans of all military services and in all components. Post-traumatic stress is real.

FM 18-66 should be required reading for any leadership development program in any sector of our society -- corporate, not-for-profit, government, and military.

Major General Byron S. Bagby, US Army (Retired)

DEDICATION

To all Americans, whether familiar with the military or not, and particularly to those who have worn our country's uniforms and their families, these life stories are for you

ACKNOWLEDGMENTS

There are far too many soldiers to acknowledge, and I have accepted that I am unable to name them all and will live with that regret. In some stories, the names are fictional, but the events are true. Several of the characters mentioned are no longer living. Primarily, I acknowledge the NCOs, officers, and soldiers of C Co. 97th Signal Battalion (1980-1983), Coleman Barracks, West Germany.

I can name them by their rank when I knew them: LTC King, LTC Clegg, Maj. Peyton, CPT Snook, SFC Lutz, SFC Brooks, SFC Turner, SFC Davis (motor pool), SFC London, 1SG Ignacio, Lieutenants Mark Bockes, Mike Fetterman, Ted Davis, Ted Young, Calvin Lawyer, Vicki Carter, CPT Harry, CPT Mary Fuller, CPT Bombaugh, SSG Boutwell, SSG Butler, Sergeants Cappa, BW Wilson, Luth, Wells, Goings, Montgomery, the company football team, the motor pool, SFC L'Heureux, Colonel Fitz-Ens, Colonel Kunde, and the list remains incomplete.

I acknowledge my son, whose first years of life, like mine, started with his father in the Army. I'm glad he never served (he's 6'4") because I used to worry about him being too big a target on any battlefield, but he has found a way to serve by coaching young men in middle school sports teams and teaching where needed.

Of course, I acknowledge my little sister, Joni, who shared Army life as a sibling with me and our mother, who kept things going even while our father spent 1965-1966 in Vietnam.

INTRODUCTION

In WWI, it was common for British and US soldiers to spend a few days in the trenches, and then a few days in the rear. That practice has endured. The time exchanging gunfire is low. Prior to combat, all soldiers spend their time before the war practicing their fighting skills—all of it. As a soldier during the Cold War, I spent my entire seven years in training, having never fired a weapon in anger. This book is not about fire and maneuver, battlefields, and foxholes, stories well-loved by most of us. Instead, these stories reveal narratives of life, of maturing as a soldier. "Everyone grows up." They say. "Time heals everything." "Idle hands are the devil's workshop." Those clichés replayed throughout our lives are partially true. For example, I learned (eventually) that busy people create less disruption than those with time on their hands; I got in more trouble at school when I was bored than the other kids who were not.

I've discovered that everyone who lives gets older, but growing up is just an option and that process requires healing. Healing? Indeed. The body wants to heal, which takes time but is not possible without effort. Emotional healing requires intention and will, a conscious decision to heal.

I was eighteen when I first put on the ROTC uniform. I started writing this book fifteen years ago, at the age of fifty-one. That makes me sixty-six now, eighteen then, sixty-six now, which is how I chose the subtitle Field Manual 18-66.When I conceived the idea for this book, very few people used Twitter; no one except a handful of college students had ever heard of Facebook, and the iPhone 4 was Apple's most advanced version. During that time, as with all eras, the cycle of life revolved. Birthing, breathing, working, dying, and so on continued. While technology changed, we aged, children grew, and life brought new experiences. The wheel continues to turn, "and it can't slow down." Life continues as Robert Frost told us: "In three words I can sum up everything I've learned about life: it goes on." Now, I'm older, a bit wiser, and remain a work in progress, still not done, not quite finished yet. Like combat boots, the polish has been applied; I've got some sheen, but parts remain tarnished, blemishes past the prime of shining. Pounded by the elements and shaped by events (my first wife divorced me, and my second wife made me a widower), I've got nooks, crags, shine, and experience—and so do you. The familiarity of common experience bonds us. This experience exists among those who wore a military uniform regardless of rank, decade of service, or branch of service.

The Army is part of my story, not all of it. I continue to love being a father, which is my greatest joy. I wasn't a father when I joined the Army, but I was when I left. Matthew was born at Eisenhower Army Medical Center at (then) Fort Gordon, Georgia, while I attended the

Signal Officer's Advanced Course. I credit the US Army with much, including its contribution to my fatherhood! (It cost $10 for his birth.) Although I was a soldier, with the different missions that entailed, commonality exists between the Army, Navy, Marine Corps, and Air Force. Everyone shared the experience of having a boss, following protocol, being told what to wear, and so on. This book is for you, too. One notable point I want to express before continuing is my respect for the US Coast Guard (USCG), technically not part of the Department of Defense but extremely professional, competent, highly trained, and among the most committed American men and women you'd find anywhere else. The USCG doesn't just train; every day, their mission is a reality. The Merchant Marine, though mainly staffed by civilians, operates the US Navy's Military Sealift Command (MSC) ships, transporting supplies to our forces "In Peace and War" (as their flag proclaims), and is just as committed to America. If you served in the military, including the USCG, and Merchant Marine, married a military spouse, or were parented by a member of the US armed forces, you will find at least one element of my life is like yours, and hopefully, you and I will connect as human beings, even if we don't know each other. If so, the US Army has now affected your life, another gift from Uncle Sam.

I've been a member of many things, sports teams, community organizations like the Lions and Chamber of Commerce, churches, a band, clubs, and a lifelong fraternity (ΦA Brothers and Little Sisters). Like many, I finished high school and unimpressively finished college, but besides fatherhood, the US Army impacted my life the greatest. I completed seven years on active duty and then served two in the Army Reserve, but no organization has impacted my life more than our fine Army. Not school, not clubs, not churches, not employers, not

Republicans, not Democrats. Nothing has influenced my daily life and values as everlastingly as the US Army.

That's not to say I discarded those other elements. Religion, Judeo-Christianity, affects my life daily. Still, those helpful organizations can lose their sense of mission by arguing about types of chairs to purchase next year, establishing a building fund, and not welcoming the new-comer while ignoring those in need. Indeed, my employer and political parties affect me, but they have not guided me in how to live my life or given me wisdom. The Army has, and that's what this book is about.

Now, what follows I have primarily written in chronological order. Broadly, it follows the timeline set out below, but each story stands on its own merit.

i. Childhood
ii. Reserve Officer Training (ROTC) resulting in commissioning
iii. Signal Corps Officer's Basic Course, Ft. Gordon, GA, Assignment to C Company, 97th Signal Battalion in Germany
iv. Signal Officer's Advanced Course, Ft. Gordon, Georgia
v. Assignment to Washington, DC
vi. Separated from Service
vii. Reserve Assignment to End of Time in Service (ETS)

Within this timeline I experienced many lessons *I needed to survive in life.*

Chapter 1

First Years

Where've you been? Where are you now? Where are you heading? We often ask and get asked questions like those, maybe even daily. All three questions are great to ponder. Being able to supply an answer you're proud of makes life easier. During those times in life when things aren't going as well, trying to answer those typical questions isn't as easy.

It's difficult, if not impossible, to know where you have been unless you look back. Failing to recognize the context of your past mistakes and successes as you look into the future encourages aimless living. The present and how you're living now is the thread that connects the past to the future. We are the point between the past and the future. Consider the flight of an arrow. If it is fired from its placement on a steady bow (the image of one's past), then the arrow travels precisely. It's the constant balance of a solid bow that propels the arrow's aim. Our past is the bow, our future the arrow. Without a solid understanding of one's past, the flight of an aimless arrow is a wobbly arc at best. Looking back also brings understanding, as we learn from historians. One of the best examples of a story about looking back occurs in the oldest part of the Bible, the Old Testament.

The Rabbis refer to the discovery of fine points of significance not directly mentioned in the Old Testament as "drashing," from the word "midrash," meaning exposition or interpretation. One of my favorite stories appears in Exodus 33, where Moses spoke with God. Moses asked the Lord to stay with his tribe as they traveled. Then he begged a second favor: "…now show me your Glory." The Lord answered, "He will cause His goodness to pass in front of Moses," but then God said, "You cannot see my face, for no one may see me and live" [NIV verse 20]. Then, in verses 22–23, the Lord told Moses that he would put him "in a cleft in the rock and cover you with my hand until I have passed by. Then I will remove my hand and you will see my back; but my face must not be seen." A lesson, a "drash" if you will, is that we are blind to seeing God at work in the present and we see his goodness only after he has walked past. Other commentaries note that by placing Moses in a cleft (some think it's a cave), light only comes in obliquely through a narrow slit, a poetic way of saying we can't see the complete truth. If Moses were not looking, he would have missed seeing God completely. The probability is high that there are truths in our own experiences that we might not see because we, preoccupied with routine living, don't look. Now that my military experiences are behind me, like God and Moses, I am looking to see what truths I might have missed.

That being said, it is not my purpose to provide a story and then show God at work in each one (He does that); instead, I share some lessons from Army life. It is also not my intention to recount the history of the US Army. Still, I must proudly say that it is the oldest military organization in the United States, founded 250 years ago in 1775. Its history is fascinating, not only as a study of strategy and tactics but also in shaping Americans' attitudes. Two hundred and fifty years ago, "then," the Continental Congress formed the US Army. I write about "then" and "now," and you're reading about it. "Then and Now." We are connected to 1775, you and I, and there is no way around it! That year directly affects all of us—those who wore the uniform and those who have not, those who recognize the effect and those who won't. Call it a mystery of life if you will, but now you are being affected by what happened then.

I first experienced the US Army as a child, having been born in 1958 during my father's senior year of ROTC at the University of Illinois. My earliest memories are of his days in the Army. It wasn't until 1966, the year he returned from Vietnam, that I knew my father as anything other than a soldier. That same year, he left the Army and enrolled in the Presbyterian Seminary in Louisville, KY, alongside another officer he had served with.

As a small boy, I didn't think of my father as being in the Army. When he came home at the end of the day, my sister and I would race to pull off his boots. Why that was fun to us is beyond me, but it was. I noticed he often wore green during those years in Germany. I don't recall seeing him at breakfast or getting ready for work. No doubt, my sister and I were still sleeping when he left.

In a rock-throwing battle, at the age of five or six, with my playground friends in Bad Kreuznach, I caught a rock on my elbow, fracturing it. My father picked me up in his roofless army jeep and sat me beside the large FM radio. Most little boys are mesmerized by army equipment, and I couldn't have been happier than on a carousel. That ride thrilled me so much, making me feel proud, like a "big boy" with his dad on the way to collect his Purple Heart. I don't even remember my arm hurting! At the infirmary, the doctor asked if I wanted a white sling or an army green one. Guess which one I chose? Yep, olive drab "o.d. green" all the way, and I returned home proud of my wound, looking forward to showing it off around the playground.

Another early memory is running with my dad to the barbershop. He was singing a Jody (a chant between a leader and formation while moving): "Here We Go... How Far?... All The Way." I doubt I ran far, maybe just to the end of our building, but it stands out as one of my memories from kindergarten. Assigned to the 8th ID Airborne Brigade during a unit "field day" (a unit-wide picnic), my mother, sister, and I watched as he and the rest of his company jumped from a C-130 air drop in Germany. The C-130 flew overhead, and as we watched, black spots emerged from the sides of the aircraft. Soon, the parachutes, resembling the capital letter D on its back, opened, bringing soldiers, our fathers, to the ground safely. Not many kids can boast about their father. I can. Unquestionably, the US Army played a significant role in shaping my early years.

Later in boyhood, after he became a civilian, I heard my father and uncles talk of their days in the Army. Some hated it outright; others considered making it their career, but for family reasons did not. One uncle had been in the Navy, another in the Marine Corps, but no one in my family liked it enough to stay twenty years. Two uncles were soldiers in WWII in the Pacific, and another served in the Korean War. One uncle, my father's brother, often said he would have stayed if he could have trusted those appointed above him in rank.

I loved their stories and didn't mind hearing them repeated. I continued to ask them questions so I could listen to their stories until they were well into their 70s. They were glad to do so until the day they died. I enjoyed hearing them, and they liked telling them.

I don't know what rank Uncle Oscar held during WWII, but overseas in the Pacific, he learned that our Aunt Grace had given birth to his son, my cousin Ernie, who is Grandma and Grandpa's first grandchild. He mentioned to his platoon leader that his wife had a baby. Expecting congratulations, the lieutenant asked Uncle Oscar if he knew "who the father was?" Uncle Oscar punched the officer in the mouth and said he thought he would get court-martialed, but the lieutenant realized he was at fault, and things were resolved satisfactorily.

What is it about the military, not just the Army, that those who served recall their memories so fondly? Is it the memory of youth? Being fit? Being away from home? Perhaps it's all of those things. Feeling nostalgic about youth is probably universal, as the poet Robert Herrick reminded us in the seventeenth century:

"That age is best which is the first
When youth and blood are warmer;"

After all, we know youth does not make a round trip: you only pass through it once. Most of us wish we could have it back, but only with the wisdom we have today.

Besides youth, it's also the adventure of experiencing something new. Thrown together with people you just met, in a place you've never been before, even sharing only English, youth, and an agreement with the government, can be a unifying experience. Set apart from society, everyone doing the same work towards the same goal is life changing.

Yep, everything I needed to survive in life, I learned from the US Army, and now I want to share more of those lessons with you.

Chapter 2

Cooperate Graduate

It surprises me today to realize how many life lessons I learned from ROTC before going on active duty. Perhaps the transition from family dependence to self-reliance explains this.

My circumstances: My family was upper lower class, unlike most of the other ROTC students, many of whom had their own bank accounts. I was seventeen; they were eighteen. I had long hair, wore T-shirts, and tennis shoes. They were clean-cut, wore polos and topsiders. I showed up at Westminster College in Fulton, MO, to the ROTC offices with hair down to my shoulders. I was overweight, and an otherwise plain-looking teenager. Either way, we all learned lessons from those in uniform.

Lieutenant Colonel Ned P. Digh was one of them. I had applied for a four-year ROTC scholarship. I went before the review board, of which LTC Digh, the senior military officer on campus, was the president. He asked me if I had been old enough to be drafted, would I have gone to Vietnam? I answered, "I don't know, and I still don't know if we should have been in Vietnam or not."

For those of you who have no family members who served in Vietnam, my seventeen-year-old answer to those who did was hurtful. I didn't know it then, not until I was in the Army and had an overdue conversation later with my Vietnam veteran father. Would LTC Digh just dismiss me as a punk kid who didn't know what he was talking about? No such luck. And I didn't get a scholarship, but LTC Digh still taught me two other lessons while in ROTC. He remained faithful to his duty to train me, even if he didn't like my attitude.

On one particular day, a few others and I were complaining about something that made absolutely no sense to us. It was such a trivial matter that I don't even remember what it was. It wouldn't be hard to imagine our grievances. The Army is known for making its soldiers hurry up and wait or for moving rocks from one place to another and then moving some back again—annoying tasks like that. Something along those lines had occurred that completely baffled a group of college kids. What happened is unimportant; how LTC Digh responded is what I want to highlight.

Colonel Digh let the following words roll off his tongue and into our ears. They've remained with me ever since: "It's just part of the game that's got to be played." In other words, he couldn't defend the reason why, but he knew it had to be done, like it or not. This was his way of telling us exactly that.

Have you ever been in a situation at work, or perhaps in your personal life, where you knew something that had to be done was irrational, but because of the system (which you joined), you had to "put up with it"? You had to play the game because of something that seemed arbitrary. You had to do it just because.

In my second marriage, my soon to be bride needed to replace her water heater as we prepared to sell her home. Her oldest teen daughter worked at Lowe's and enjoyed an employee discount, but she said we had to go to the Lowe's in Chantilly, which was twenty-five miles from our home in Manassas, and also twenty-five miles from her assigned store. These were her requirements because she had just split with her boyfriend and didn't want to risk seeing him, even though she wasn't sure if he was working that day.

I thought my fiancé and her daughter were joking. I did. "You cannot be serious." I protested at the silliness of this, but it soon became clearer that they were as serious as heart attacks, and they both looked at me as if I had three green eyes in the middle of my forehead. They weren't just serious; they were damn serious! Thank God I remembered LTC Digh's advice: "It's just part of the game that's got to be played." It helped me. I stopped myself from going on and on about how stupid it was, and stopped complaining, "I can't believe we are doing this." We got into my truck, drove to Chantilly, picked up the water heater, and brought it back. I let it go and never mentioned it again.

The other lesson he taught was "Cooperate, Graduate." I know it doesn't apply as precisely as other lessons, but its broad general theme of getting along as a team is valuable. Cooperation is undoubtedly preferable to obstruction. He used that phrase about Army schools. His experience as an infantry ranger officer gave him that wisdom. He learned the importance of cooperation, the wisdom of not making life more difficult for others than it has to be, and realizing your opinion is not the holiest of all views.

"Cooperate, Graduate" got me through my stint at Microsoft, where on day one, the hiring manager advised us: "You cannot get done in eight hours what we expect you to. The sooner you accept that, the happier you'll be." They were up front with us from the very start, within the first few hours of our first day. I decided right then I wouldn't complain about not being paid enough for the number of hours I would have to work. "Cooperate, Graduate." Cooperation goes a long way in the workplace, and it was lacking in many of my work experiences after leaving the military. Perhaps you have worked with some whiners or a group that thinks everyone else is stupid, so they refuse to do things they disagree with, even when the boss orders it. Or they get loud and make sure everyone else knows how right they are. It's quite draining. I hope you aren't in that kind of environment. Once that negativity becomes the central cultural definition, it isn't easy to break. People get comfortably stuck in their habits.

"Cooperate, Graduate" does not require one to stay quiet and go along to get along. That's anathema to the Army, where "yes men" are ridiculed and rarely do well, but once the discussion has ended it's time to march, and THAT is where the cooperation begins.

At work, I used to go around the office and say: "Cooperate, Graduate." If it did nothing else, it enabled me to get along well enough to survive the office politics, and that was good enough!

Cooperate, Graduate. Try it! See how it works for you!

Chapter 3

Uncle Phil

During the sophomore year at Westminster College, students were forced to leave the freshman quadrangle and move elsewhere. I chose the Sigma Alpha Epsilon SAE fraternity house. Typically, 75 percent of this all-men's school pledged to join a fraternity, while the other 25 percent were either on athletic scholarships, which prohibited frat life, or just despised fraternities. As freshmen, our suite mates were often Sigma Chis, Betas, Phi-Delts, Independents, etc. "ROTC," as we were called, was not segregated and we lived among the student body at large.

In the SAE house, we had a day cook. He was an older Black gent, a former boxer, with biceps the size of my calves. His last name was Phillips; we called him "Uncle Phil" for short. Uncle Phil stood about five feet nine and walked bowlegged, a walk we all viewed as a swagger. Uncle Phil was a Korean War veteran, in the anti-aircraft artillery, Quad-50s, similar to the ones Jane Fonda sat on in North Vietnam. We, the new students in the house, were afraid of him and tried not to interact with him. During my first year in the house, I landed on his wrong side.

Uncle Phil sweated profusely while working in the windowless corner over the grill and stove, so he kept the back door, opposite his end of the kitchen, open. One cold Missouri morning, I strolled into the kitchen for breakfast and said, "It's cold in here, close that door!" I walked over and shut it. HA HA HA. Instead of laughing, Uncle Phil flashed me a look that said he wanted to carve my liver. He reopened that door, informing me it was never to be closed again except at his command. For the next three years, his assistant, A.C., teased me, trying to stir the pot by telling me to "Go close that door, it's cold in here!" Uncle Phil would look at me with a death stare, waiting to pounce, while A.C. laughed away.

Breakfast wasn't a sit-down meal. You just walked into Uncle Phil's domain and asked if it was possible to have pancakes or eggs (most of us wanted to know beforehand if Uncle Phil's mood was anti-pancakes or anti-eggs that morning). One of the politest guys in the house irritated the heck out of Uncle Phil. Every morning, Tom would come in and say: "Good morning, Mr. Phillips, may I have some pancakes, please?" It wasn't so much Tom's politeness as it was how he said it: mealy-mouthed. That approach irritated Uncle Phil. It was as if Tom knew Uncle Phil couldn't quarrel with politeness, and in turn, Uncle Phil got annoyed because he knew Tom knew that. "No, Mr. Billings, you may not have pancakes this morning; today we have eggs." It was fun for me to watch Uncle Phil while I ate. I spent many mornings doing just that.

Then, when Uncle Phil realized I was in ROTC, his attitude towards me changed. I wasn't just another White punk in a Republican school of privileged kids waiting for him to cook his meals. Over my three years, he and I spoke often, one-on-one. It impressed him to hear me play along with George Benson on my guitar, and he'd laugh when I couldn't keep up with the Maestro. I'd put my guitar down and shake my head incredulously, amazed at Benson's skill.

My decision to join the Army meant something to Uncle Phil. Another guy in the house, a year ahead of me, enrolled in ROTC, and Uncle Phil started doing us small but noticeable favors. He would put a little extra cheese in my omelet or make me one straightaway, sensing I wanted one but didn't want to ask. He appreciated my respect for him. The Army, which I hadn't entered yet, created a bridge between our age and race, allowing us to communicate in ways that were closed off to the other boys in the house.

He also liked me because I would argue with him. We bantered about the Right-to-Work amendment; I was against it, and he was for it. We argued whether Carter should be president or Ford, or philosophically whether or not truth was always logical, or even if the local judge should be reelected. I used to look for things to discuss with him that I was sure he would oppose. It was fun for both of us.

Uncle Phil spoke words to me one morning that I've not forgotten. We were talking about the Army, and I can still see him swinging a big soup pot up on the counter as he said them. Even though I didn't fully comprehend what he meant back in 1978, I've held onto his words: "**The Army will make you a man or keep you a boy**."

I thought of his words many times after commissioning.

At the Basic Course for Second Lieutenants, the school called us together in a conference room. Happily, President Carter had just announced an across-the-board 11 percent pay increase for the military. That was huge news! We all chatted excitedly about it. A lieutenant colonel asked us, as a group, if we had any concerns, etc. One officer raised his hand and asked: "Sir, the 11 percent raise is awesome, but the price of combat boots just went up from $35 to $60 (we were required to have two pairs.) Uniforms also went up, so the 11 percent hardly covers the price increases, and what are they going to do about that?"

I felt bad for this officer. He embarrassed himself, and didn't know it. I thought to myself: the days of entitlement were in the past, and this was Uncle Phil's words coming to life: "The Army will make you a man or keep you a boy."

Short of a lobotomy, I'll never forget Uncle Phil. My admiration for him has not diminished, and I've got the US Army to thank for knowing him. To this day, I don't remember his first name, and a search on the internet leaves me empty-handed. I wish I had thanked him. After I joined, I never saw him again, and I regret it, one of those lifelong regrets I still carry. Wherever he is, I hope it's peaceful.

Update Memorial Day 2025.

After I recalled his first name, another search for Uncle Phil delivered this result:

Chapter 4

Cutting Corners

One of the better lessons I learned from the Army happened before I was commissioned, still a youthful college-boy ROTC cadet. It was also a painful lesson because it has to be called upon when the tough, terrible times arrive, and for that reason, it just outright sucks. Nevertheless, this lesson has served me well, and it's one that everyone should embrace.

In ROTC, the first two years require no commitment from Uncle Sam. They paid me nothing, funded none of my tuition, and I had no contract. The commitment becomes serious once the third year begins. We drew $100 a month, and during the summer between our junior and senior years, we were required to attend six weeks at an ROTC Advanced Camp. Our school was assigned to Fort Riley, Kansas.

As a junior, we would leave the tutelage of Captain (CPT) Stephenson, in charge of the freshmen and sophomores, and move beneath the steely watchful eyes of Captain Ron Phillips (no relation to "Uncle Phil.")

CPT Phillips was serious and intense, and everyone was afraid of him. Hailing from Alabama, from my perspective as a kid from from the Chicago area, before getting to know him, his regional roots added to my fear. Neil Young sang about Alabama and the Southern Man, then Lynyrd Skynyrd rallied with "Sweet Home Alabama." The South had Sergeant York, Rod Steiger's character Chief Gillespie from *In the Heat of the Night*, the beatings at the Edmund Pettis bridge, Robert E. Lee, and George Wallace. All this created a certain trepidation in me, the Northerner.

CPT Phillips was an Airborne Ranger and a commissioned Infantry Officer, and like almost everyone in the Army at that time, he was a Vietnam veteran. After the war, he was branch-transferred against his will to the Military Police (MP) Corps, which meant he came to us as an MP. It's a stereotype, but there's a perception that MPs enjoyed hurting people. Additionally, he was a Southern cop with all the stereotypes that entails. On top of that, CPT Phillips was White. Not just Caucasian: he was white, as if the sun never darkened his skin, no matter how long he stood in it, as if he flipped the sun off and told it to leave him alone. CPT Phillips was a Billy-BadAss: Southerner, MP, Vietnam vet, Airborne Ranger, and former Infantry Officer competent in patrolling and tactics, and fit. His age? I don't know, maybe in his early 30s, married with kids. That didn't matter to us.

Captain Phillips was relentless when it came to physical training (PT). He trained people well. Little did we know that one of his cadets from the class of 1978 would become a two-star general (Major General) and the Assistant Division Commander of the 10th Mountain Division, Byron Bagby. Also, under his leadership, the class ahead of me completed their Advanced Camp and returned home with the Commander's Trophy, outperforming every school that sent cadets to Fort Riley. That class had the highest scores in the PT Test, range qualification, land navigation, and military skills. Everyone in that group in '79 earned the "recondo badge," granting them the right to wear a special badge on their cadet uniform pocket for all to see. Recondo means little or nothing to the Army, but in ROTC, it was a distinguishing honor one could achieve. For a small private college to win the Commander's Trophy in 1979 was a remarkable achievement, especially considering that Texas A&M, the largest of the six military colleges in the US, remains the New York Yankees of the Commander's Trophy. Typically, 60 percent of their student body are members of the "Corps of Cadets" with ROTC programs for the Army, Navy, and Air Force. Each year, they send fifty to seventy cadets to ROTC Summer Camp. Our Westminster class of 1980 had twelve.

As sophomores not yet under CPT Phillips' tutelage, we knew he was serious about PT We watched what he put the class ahead of us through: two hours of morning PT before school started, which included long-distance runs in combat boots, hand-to-hand combat, and continual extracurricular work. He told us flat out he wanted the Commander's Trophy returned to Westminster College.

CPT Phillips wanted the Commander's Trophy, and I was a Northerner—naive and never really physically challenged, even though I lettered in tennis. Now, I find myself overweight, looking nothing like the lean, mean fighting machine he needed. So, I began my third year of ROTC, no longer a teenager and moving closer to adulthood.

The first semester, August to December, with CPT Phillips wasn't bad at all. We wondered what the fuss was all about. We worked with him in the classroom. He taught us skills that I have used throughout my adult life, map reading, land navigation, orienteering, patrolling, platoon tactics in the offense and defense, setting fields of fire, calling in artillery support, how to plan, and leadership.

During one winter field training exercise (FTX), it was incredibly cold. The Missouri windchill dipped into the single digits that weekend. We shivered as we patrolled through the fields and woods, carrying our M-16s and equipment, ill-prepared for that kind of chill. We pulled our fingers out of our gloves and tucked them into our palms, using them as mittens to keep warm. We walked, ensuring we bent our toes to maintain blood flow. CPT Phillips was right there with us, and I never saw him shiver or show any sign of cold. We just figured he was reptilian and could adapt better to the chill than we could. It was a struggle not to complain, but I managed, and we all did well, grateful to be on the leeward side of a ridge or behind a tree when sheltered from the wind. I was impressed that he seemed unbothered by the cold. That FTX was just a familiarization, an Army experience added to our training. Patrolling was no longer just academic; you could truly feel it. The best training combines intellect and emotions!

During the first semester, he had each of us teach a military skills subject. It was good practice for standing in front of a crowd as an authority on a topic, making us somewhat of an expert in our subject area. That was fun. I learned a lot and still have my notebook from those classes. The first semester wasn't as bad with CPT Phillips as we had imagined. Then the second semester came, and so did the PT.

Our first training session was in the gymnasium in January, the same building where Winston Churchill gave his world-famous Iron Curtain speech: "From Stettin, in the Baltic, to Trieste in the Adriatic, an Iron Curtain has descended across the Continent...." In 1979, every American had heard of and knew about the Iron Curtain speech.

Some historians argue that those words started the Cold War. Thirty-three years later, America was still in the middle of it, and my colleagues and I began getting in shape to continue fighting that war; I was in the same place where Churchill declared it, and that made my work feel global.

Gymnasium, Westminster College, Fulton, MO

PT started at 6 a.m. ("0600 hours"). We wore our uniforms and tennis shoes to the nationally registered historic landmark gym. We did the assigned set of calisthenics, executed by the numbers, with one of us leading PT.

You might think it's relatively easy to get a group to exercise in unison. There were three different sets of calisthenics, each with about seven different exercises. As the leader, you had to give the commands to get the cadets into PT formation: "Extend to the Left, MOVE!" With each exercise, you also had to explain how it was to be executed. "You will go to your left, and I will go to my right, thus creating a mirror image." All of this had to be memorized. Then you did a demonstration of each exercise.

The leader of PT also had to count every movement of the exercise, while the students only counted the number of completed repetitions. Ever tried talking and doing calisthenics at the same time? It will challenge your physical fitness and lung capacity, your brain and body!

The most difficult of the three conditioning drills was set #2, which included the eight-count push-up. The exercise began in the upright position, "hands down by your side, feet spread shoulder width apart." The command to begin was "Starting Position, MOVE!" The formation came to attention.

"In cadence, EXERCISE!" You dropped your butt and put your hands out in front of you, "ONE," the leader yelled.

On the count of two, you thrust your legs "vigorously" behind you. "TWO" "THREE" lower your chest just an inch or two above the ground. On "FOUR," return with your arms straightened, completing the push-up. "FIVE" lower your chest back towards the ground again.

"SIX" return to the "front leaning rest position."

"SEVEN" bring your feet back beneath your butt close to your hands, and on the final count, the other cadets sounded off with the number of reps just completed: "ONE," and so on until you did twelve repetitions of this most hated exercise.

When it was my turn to lead PT, CPT Phillips ensured I led drill #2 with the eight-count push-up. He knew no one wanted to lead set #2 because it was the toughest. I never said a word about it; it had to be done, and that was that. Besides being winded from just doing the exer-cise, counting the set of twelve out loud resulted in further fatigue. I suspect, to this day, that CPT Phillips made sure I always drew PT drill #2 for that reason.

After the calisthenics, CPT Phillips ran us in formation. We were inside the gym, in fatigues, and he told us he would increase our distance and time as the year went on, to where we would run to the airport in formation, a six-mile trip. For our first two training runs, we ran for ten minutes straight without stopping.

The Eight-Count Push-Up

Round and round the gym we ran. As a heavier individual, I wasn't ready to run like the deer he needed me to become. He told us not to cut corners, stay outside the red line, off the basketball court. He knew that running around the corners meant a longer distance for us. Soon, I started to cut the square and tried to make the pattern more circular without getting caught. In their architectural style, Asians prefer round curves to square blocks for lines, why couldn't I apply that style now? I decided to take off the edges, to "round out the turn," and began making our square pattern a circle, literally "cutting corners." I would still run ten minutes, but less distance and just a smidgen slower.

CPT Phillips caught me. "Aww, Stahlman, you're cutting corners. Get down and start knocking 'em out!" I got down and started doing push-ups to atone for my crime, guilty as charged. He barked: "I didn't tell you to begin." I could see I was being made the example, and I knew all I could do was play my part. He ordered me to put my feet up on the bleachers, hands on the floor, which I did.

I followed through with what I knew he wanted: "Permission to begin, sir?" I shouted.

"Begin!" he ordered. I did ten push-ups. "Stahlman, I didn't hear you count."

"Permission to begin again, Sir?"

"Begin!"

"One Sir, Two Sir" all the way to ten.

"Permission to recover, Sir?"

"Recover!" At which time I came to attention and ran to catch my classmates.

The ten minutes went by, and we made it. I tested CPT Phillips, and he slammed me, forced me to do push-ups, and refused to let me "get by." After we were dismissed, we all chuckled about me doing push-ups; these were my bragging rights. I was the first to drop, to run through that entire sequence of permission, and to elevate my feet while doing push-ups. He made an example of me. I led the way! Ha ha ha.

I never cut corners again after that.

What a powerful lesson: "Don't cut corners!" Literally and figuratively, that morning in the gym was a lesson for the rest of my life. Ever buy a home where the roofer "cut corners"? What about when you cut corners on the amount of your charitable giving, your relationship with your spouse, or the work you produce? Cheating. It has consequences. I got off easily that morning. Twenty push-ups cost me very little, but I pay a higher price when I cut corners today. Cutting corners in nutrition leads to high blood pressure, obesity, and heart issues. Cutting corners on tax reporting can land you in prison. Perhaps you own a construction company, and if you "cut corners" with cheap concrete bolts on an underwater tunnel project, parts of the ceiling could collapse, causing traffic to be disrupted. Sometimes I cut corners when it comes to dusting and ironing. Cutting corners is self-indulgent and lacks discipline.

Once you admit you've cut corners, the best thing to do next is stop, take what's coming, and correct yourself.

The Army taught me that, and when and if I cut corners today, I regret it.

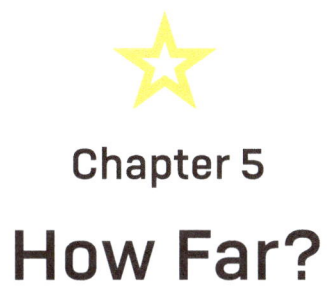

Chapter 5

How Far?

Cutting corners is really about seeking happiness. In my example, I believed I would be happier running a shorter distance than a longer distance. So I tried it and proved my assumption wrong. I learned how to restrain my base desire, to "stifle" it and thereby avoid the unhappiness that cutting corners guarantees and did what I was expected to.

And I was happier!

Aristotle taught that a fundamental requirement for happiness is to live virtuously, to "do the right thing." He didn't say "do the right thing according to you," nor did he say, "according to your situation, finances, mood, or whatever." That's all good and fine, isn't it, as long as your family isn't falling apart, you have enough money, and work is going tolerably well? What did the Army teach me about life when things are tough?

That lesson, too, came from CPT Phillips and is probably the greatest lesson I've ever learned.

After a month or so of running in the gym three days a week, CPT Phillips moved us outside to begin an hour long daily morning run that was increased to two hours by the end of the school year.

We ran in boots. We ran in fatigues, sometimes in T-shirts, sometimes with rubberized training weapons, and sometimes with field gear. I was bigger than most of my peers. I weighed two hundred pounds at six feet tall, but I would say most of my peers were in the one-hundred-sixty-pound range and a few inches shorter. I wasn't built to run, but I had to.

We had a "mascot" that ran with us. It wasn't a dog or a horse, just an eighteen inch by eighteen inch wooden box painted red with the Army Ranger tab on one side, silver Airborne Wings on the other, and two black boot prints painted on top. There were holes drilled in the sides of the box through which yellow nylon rope looped to serve as carrying handles.

Wherever we went, The Mascot went.

For our first arrival on Priest Field, the Westminster College athletic field, we were immediately told, "Thou shalt not walk upon my field." We started running to our meeting point as soon as our first boot hit the grass. The Mascot was by the PT leader's side.

If we moved to the other end of the field, we better not leave the Mascot behind. We treated it as one of us. When it came time to line up in formation to prepare for that morning's run, nobody grabbed The Mascot. We then discovered the real reason for the yellow ropes.

CPT Phillips required us to run in a two-man-wide column formation, with two of us carrying The Mascot between us at all times. We were incredulous and thought he was asking us to do the absurd for no other reason than to harass us. It felt pointless, silly, and evil, confirming our opinion of MPs. We didn't protest, though, and two of us grabbed The Mascot, one holding it with their right hand and another with their left as we marched until the command of "Double Tiiiiiiiiiime, MARCH!" We moved from marching to running, lugging the Mascot with us. We did it without complaint because we knew complaining wouldn't help

The Mascot offered no real lessons, except perhaps that we shared the burden it created and took turns carrying the load collectively. That is a valuable lesson sculpted for the Army, and one I've missed since leaving the military. Rarely have I encountered such a willingness to prioritize mission over self, outside of Army life. Minimizing individual importance for the common good is uncommon in American society.

In my civilian occupation, it's rare to see that trait, the willingness to accept difficult experiences or tasks. Usually, what I hear is: "I ain't doing that!" or "They don't pay ME enough to do that."

Sometimes in my own work life, I have felt that way, especially when I perceived the company couldn't care less about my needs. In the Army, it can be generally said that leaders care about soldiers. They care about job assignments and how they align with career progression. Leaders, I mean good leaders, care about their soldiers' promotions, and they certainly care about the soldiers' home life.

I knew CPT Phillips, an experienced leader, was training us for future responsibilities. In essence, he was taking care of our needs. So we picked up The Mascot and ran together in formation. We passed it back and forth, up and down the formation to our peers in front of us and back to peers behind us whenever we tired of carrying the burden.

Guys like me, who couldn't run worth a hoot, would eventually drop out of formation, leaving the decreasing number of cadets to carry The Mascot. I tried not to drop out, but invariably, at some point during the run, I would. I wasn't cutting corners; I didn't drop out because I wanted to get away with something (that ended with the lesson in the gym). I ran slower because I "couldn't hang;" I was out of shape. Those who dropped out had to keep running; we never stopped. We were just slower. We were indeed being trained to run faster, to run longer. The formation continued onward. Eventually, CPT Phillips would order the main group to "double column," executing two ninety-degree turns, now running towards us to "pick up the stragglers." As they passed us, we would rejoin the formation and resume running at their pace, until it happened again.

I didn't want to drop out, and soon I got to where I wasn't the first to drop out.

Later in the afternoon, CPT Phillips required remedial PT for anyone who dropped out that morning. Remedial participants also included those who had not yet scored at least a seventy on each test in the Army's five-event PT Test. The Army required sixty points per event, but Ranger School and Recondo required seventy, so CPT Phillips made that his standard. The horizontal ladder and running were my weakest events. My poor performance, or dropping out of a run, meant I would be doing two-a-days at Priest Field on Monday, Wednesday, and Friday, until the last month of the school year, when it became every day.

I ran longer and faster as training continued, but the main group ran further and quicker too! I would invariably fall back, but at later points than previously. It was a challenging time for me, because of my size, but I had the bones and height the Good Lord gave me, and that was that.

I applied some mental challenges my father taught me. I would pick a spot towards which we were running, a telephone pole, a fire hydrant, or a parked car, and tell myself, *If I can only make it there…* Then, reaching that point, I would pick another spot and do the same thing. Sometimes I would look at the boots of the person in front of me, and since we ran in step, I would pretend their boots were tied to mine, like train wheels, in unison pulling me forward. It was a mind game, but I was still dropping out.

When we started in the gym, CPT Phillips told us we would run for ten minutes, then fifteen, and on to twenty, which was enough to cover the two-mile Army requirement. Once we moved outside, he never told us how far we would run or for how long. Ever.

During the school day, a few others and I stayed behind after class and talked with CPT Phillips. He invited us to discuss our training, purpose, reasons, and other related topics. He was human! We could talk to him, after all! I asked him, "Sir, why don't you ever tell us how far we are going to run?"

"If I told you how far you were going to run, you could do it."

His answer pissed me off immediately. "Sir, I want to finish a run without stopping, and you know I could do it if you told us the distance, and yet you refuse to do so?" Incredibly sadistic, I thought. "OK, then, tell me why."

Here comes the lesson.

He said, "If I can get you to beat me, then I've done my job."

My nineteen-year-old mind was stunned and curious at the same time. "What do you mean?" I asked.

"If I can get you to keep running when the end isn't in sight, and you can keep going anyway, not knowing when the discomfort will end, then you are stronger than before. That's my job."

"You're saying your goal is to see us keep running without quitting until it's over, even when we don't know when it's going to end?"

"You got it."

The light went on for me. It was a mind game. I mean, not just a mind game; the running was still there, but he wasn't just trying to beat us down. He wanted us to beat him, to make us successful, and that required not only physical strength but also mental toughness. He called it "intestinal fortitude." I didn't realize how powerful this life lesson would become.

The next morning at PT, after calisthenics, hand-to-hand combat, and other drills, we ran about a three-mile loop, a shorter distance than we had been running. We ran from Priest Field, made turns (never knowing exactly where we were going), and eventually headed back towards the campus, all in formation. No one had dropped out! We made the final turn towards Priest Field. Others and I rejoiced, thinking *the end is in sight, I've made it*! We were like stable horses returning home to the barn. The pace picked up faster, but I decided I could make it. Closer and closer we came. Every step I made meant one less second of pain, and we would be set free from this torment. We were excited at the prospect of hearing the command: "Quick Time, March!" ordering us to resume the comfortable marching pace.

We got to Priest Field. Any second now. *No, not that one, OK, when my left boot hits the ground again, surely, that will signal the end*. We kept running. *OK, two more steps and we are through, I am certain*. We kept running, past the place where we started. *What's going on? Doesn't he know we are at the starting point?* There came no command ordering us to quick time. CPT Phillips kept running. Our hope was dying; the prize we sought was being lost, ripped from us. When we realized he wasn't going to stop, half of us dropped out, more than ever before, including me, believing we couldn't go any further. CPT Phillips won again.

He was toying with us. He and the main body kept running for a few blocks more, then he turned around, and ordered quick time. We had quit too early. I could have run the extra few blocks, *If I had ONLY known*! my mind screamed. Once again, he declared checkmate in this mind game; I still hadn't beaten him.

That's perhaps the grandest lesson for life the US Army imparted to me: the willingness, the decision (notice I didn't say ability), to keep going during the tough times, when the end is unknown, only knowing that it will end, sometime.

Like running for CPT Phillips, our **troubles, though they last a long time, longer than we want or think they should, are never permanent.** Lou Holtz, the winning coach at Notre Dame, tells his audiences that he's "been on top, and he's been on bottom, and he'll be both places again." What are you going to decide in the beginning and middle of adversity?

When my ex-wife moved my son 1,000 miles away from me after a rough custody battle, I had to keep running to be the best father I could, despite my limited abilities.

When my second wife was killed in an auto accident six days before our first wedding anniversary, I had to decide to "keep on running." This is not pathological denial. The pain must be acknowledged, tourniquets applied, anger and tears expressed, but the decision to run must be made. You can quit if you want, but make sure it's not permanent. Problems, like life itself, are temporary. As God commands us to choose life, it is easier because we know it's temporary anyway.

Happiness and sadness are never permanent. Incorporating that lesson from CPT Phillips into daily life is a scary one, as I thankfully do not know what lies ahead; however, it enables me not just to believe, but to know, "this too shall pass."

Back Row, Fourth from the Left with other members of SAE.
Notice the hair parted down the middle.
(Their picture does not imply endorsement)

Chapter 6

Patrol Leader?

Eventually, I could run the two miles in less than eighteen minutes in combat boots and score at least a seventy in each of the five events of the Army fitness test. Every third-year ROTC cadet attended a six-week summer training. Across the nation, 8,000 cadets from 290 schools reported to Fort Lewis, Fort Bragg, Fort Knox, Fort Benning, or Fort Riley. We in Missouri went to Fort Riley, housed in World War I and World War II barracks without air conditioning at Camp Forsyth, which has since been converted into modern family housing. The summer high temperatures there average 90°F. Not only did CPT Phillips want us to be prepared for avoiding heat exhaustion by being fit, but CPT Phillips also trained us for Ranger School. I realize that now.

Looking back, I can see that the ROTC had its curriculum, but CPT Phillips had his own. He wanted Westminster to win the Commander's

Postcard of Camp Forsyth with WWII barracks

Trophy again, and he knew that if he could raise our baseline performance to equal the standards for admission to Ranger School, then he, our school, we, had a great chance to bring that trophy home again.

Few cadets at Fort Riley that summer of 1979 matched CPT Phillips' level of preparation. We learned hand-to-hand combat, surprising cadets from other schools. We rappelled several times a year, scaling cliffs and mostly descending from the Science Center building. Many were shocked that we did two hours of PT every morning before class. We ran six miles in boots, in formation, sometimes with rubber M-16s, and always with The Mascot. We performed push-ups in the creek that symbolically separated Priest Field from the academic buildings, elevating our feet on tree trunks, or The Mascot, or thirty-six inch tires of a deuce-and-a-half cargo truck. Under the guidance of active-duty drill sergeants, we ran the obstacle course at Fort Leonard Wood.

At school, other "civilian" students, not in ROTC, were stressed due to their classes. We carried, in addition to their burdens, the serious responsibility of learning about the US Army. It was damn good training. It, more than my degree, prepared me for life, the world, and how not to be just the academic theoretician that universities revere.

The Army always (and it's often a criticism) trains for the last war. Those who graduated from ROTC or the Academy between the 1940s and 1960s primarily learned the strategy and tactics of World War II and the Korean War. In 1979, we learned the tactics of Vietnam, which consisted of the basic components of the Patrol and the Base Camp.

There is a lot to patrolling. It's a complicated process with detailed steps when done correctly. CPT Phillips ensured we understood patrolling, by drilling it into our heads, so much so that to this day, when I see a ridge line, I think about the "military crest" of hills, or when I see an open field surrounded by a tree line, I consider how to lead a squad or platoon across it, or the creek that runs through its middle. Learning those tactics takes practice.

The Germans have a saying that "Practice Makes the Master" (Übung macht den Meister), and our Army embodies this principle. If you practice something enough, it becomes second nature. Professional athletes understand this well. NHL players don't think about skating, and NBA players know how to shoot free throws instinctively. In the Army, when your rifle jams, that's not the moment to learn how to clear it. The Army refers to that repair sequence as the "Immediate Action Drill," which outlines the steps to follow when your weapon malfunctions.

Patrolling involves many variables. Patrolling requires quiet.

Maurice Bilderback, who taught my father how to hunt, only hunted squirrels barefoot. He wouldn't hunt with anyone who wore noisy shoes. Patrolling requires your gear to be silent. You wrapped tape around the clinking parts of your ammunition pouches or web belt and jumped up and down to demonstrate that you were reasonably quiet.

When moving down the road, the patrols walk in a staggered formation, not side by side. Soldiers on the right point their barrels to the right, and members of the patrol on the left point their barrels to the left. Many things had to be learned and agreed upon before you ever left the base camp. As a member of the patrol, you needed to understand and practice all these things.

As patrol leader, you had to check and ensure your soldiers were doing what they were supposed to. "Oooops, forgot to put on camouflage" wasn't something a good patrol leader would hear while on the move! Trust, but verify. "Check, check, and re-check" remains one of the mottoes of leadership. Checking and correcting builds confidence, which in turn creates trust.

CPT Phillips had each of us practice the roles within a patrol: patrol leader, assistant patrol leader, and all the other positions. We carried a copy of the *Ranger Handbook* he issued to each of us. (I don't know if other schools required it, but he did.) The overriding standard rule of the US military is that a "Leader is responsible for everything his unit does or fails to do." This is still printed in the *Ranger Handbook* of our modern US Army today (*Makes you wish Presidents knew of this guidance, doesn't it?*).

In class, CPT Phillips would run us through hypotheticals: "You are out on patrol, and you walk into an ambush, what are you going to do now, Patrol Leader?" he would ask.

"You're patrolling in the wood line, and come to an open field, but have to get to the other side. What are you going to do now, Patrol Leader?"

"You are patrolling in wide open terrain and come under artillery fire, what are you going to do now, Patrol Leader?"

We heard that question all year long, repeatedly: "What are you going to do now, Patrol Leader?" He analyzed our answers and showed us the benefits and disadvantages of our decisions.

Then he took us out in the woods for a weekend to practice what we talked about, patrolling by day, and sleeping under the stars at night. He staged pre-planned scenarios to challenge us. Over and over, he asked us, "What are you going to do now, Patrol Leader?" and forced us to think about how to practice immediately making decisions under stress, to test our ability to incorporate our training into "right-now" application.

WHAT? What's going on? You have options, which ones are you going to consider?

WHAT ARE YOU? What are you made of? What are your values, your character?

WHAT ARE YOU GOING TO DO? Choose, you have to choose!

WHAT ARE YOU GOING TO DO NOW? And, you have to choose now!

WHAT ARE YOU GOING TO DO NOW, PATROL LEADER? Come on, boss, people are depending on you. What you decide will affect many others.

Imagine facing situations for which you never prepared. This training compelled us to practice responding to the unexpected and unforeseen.

It was terrific training, not just for patrolling, something I never had to lead while on active duty, but for life, and here I thought it was only about the Army.

It served me well.

One night, as a captain stationed at the Pentagon, I came home to an empty house and a note from my wife telling me she had taken our son and moved. I knew a divorce was coming, just not when. When stressed, we humans revert to old habits. *What are you going to do now, Patrol Leader?* danced across my mind.

I sat down on the empty kitchen floor and bawled. Then I found a local church that also sponsored a group for adults going through divorce. My pain subsided for a moment when I saw an attractive thir-ty-four-year-old woman who, seven years later, became my second wife. Another reversal hit me when she was killed in an automobile accident on her way to work during our first year of marriage. CPT Phillips' question returned to my mind: *What are you going to do now, Patrol Leader?*

I had my wife cremated and sent her ashes home with her wonderful parents after the funeral. That's what I did. I sat down and cried, many days, and worked as much as I could, then decided to move to Dallas, TX, to be near my son. It turned out to be one of the smartest decisions of my life.

CPT Phillips' question is a great challenge. I am certain he was not the one who came up with it, he heard it from someone he admired too. I think of it often, even when not faced with traumatic situations like I shared with you, but also at work, or in traffic, or when dealing with people. *What are you going to do now, Patrol Leader?* It's less a point of instruction than a technique for coping in life, which I learned from the US Army and CPT Phillips.

Next time the unexpected hits you in the face, remember your training, who you are, who loves you, and what you value. Practice it, and master it. Then, when you ask yourself, ***What are you going to do now,*** *Patrol Leader?* you'll find the answer.

I earned the Recondo badge that summer at Fort Riley, but one of my classmates did not, and the Commander's Trophy returned to Texas A&M that year.

Chapter 7

Reverse Planning

Doing things backwards doesn't come naturally. Sure, our friend in the Marine Corps, Gomer Pyle, seemed to do things backwards, Gilligan used to do most everything backwards, but none of us wanted to be like them.

It's ironic that today I still use a technique preached by the Army, and that is to plan backwards, use the reverse planning sequence.

This is Steven Covey's second habit from his book, *7 Habits of Highly Effective People*. He calls it "Begin with the end in mind." I don't know if Mr. Covey was ever in the US Army, but it doesn't matter; it's not a new concept. For centuries, it has been guidance for athletes to visualize their victory and set goals. However, it was the US Army that introduced it to me, and I give Uncle Sam the credit.

I was intrigued when CPT Phillips first told my fellow ROTC cadets and me about the "reverse planning sequence." It went against my intuition and the way I had approached every undertaking. Unlike Mr. Covey, the Army's approach makes planning complete. "Beginning with the end in mind" unifies the team to mutually agree on an outcome, a critical task. Arnold Schwarzenegger called it vision, seeing yourself as you want to become. He focuses on clear and attainable goals. That approach is perfect for setting direction and maintaining enthusiasm, but it does not uncover obstacles hidden along the way. The Reverse Planning Method concretely identifies every impediment that must be overcome for the goal to be achieved. It's the difference between having a goal and having a goal with a plan.

The Bible begins with the words of Moses in Genesis and the creation of the world. Christianity starts with the birth, not the death, of Jesus Christ [theological discussions aside]. We studied the Revolutionary War before the Civil War in high school. *Past before the present, present before the future. That's the only proper way for any rational human being to think.* I told myself. Begin backwards? It nearly shook my confidence in the captain, and soon the entire US military could have been subjected to my ridicule. "Begin by planning the ending... Indeed!"

I knew, however, that CPT Phillips had risen to Captain, graduated from Ranger School, survived Vietnam with a CIB (Combat Infantryman's Badge), and thus his assertion, no matter how silly it might have initially seemed, deserved my time and attention to hear his case.

I thought I was already good at planning, but the US Army took that further. The rule, the concept, is to define precisely what you want from a project. An example might be: I want to push the enemy from the hilltop, and then successfully defend the hilltop. Perhaps for you it could be: I want the customer to accept my product and pay their invoice. A better example is baking a cake or building a sawhorse. The last thing you might do is paint or stain the sawhorse. To do that, you must have the paint, can opener, brush, and tarp to protect from spills. Before you paint it, the sawhorse should be checked to see that it's level. To get it level, the legs have to be sawn the same length, at the same angles. To saw the legs, you have to buy the boards, which means you have to know how many to buy, etc. Get the drift? Same with a cake. To serve a cake, you may need a cake plate and a cake cover. You will need a knife, possibly a serving spatula. The cake has to come out of a pan. What kind of pan, rectangle, circular, bundt, greased, or lined with parchment? The reverse planning sequence builds solid sawhorses and bakes beautiful cakes.

What is the last thing to do in order to finish a project? Just before completion, what needs to be done to finalize it, and what is the next step before that? On and on it goes until your instruction sequence includes you at the keyboard typing the plan right where you are standing or sitting.

In the hilltop example, the last goal was to successfully defend the hilltop. In order to successfully defend that hilltop means I have to know where to put my automatic "crew-served" weapons, which squads will be assigned to what locations, where the mortars are going to go, where the platoon sergeant will be, where I and the radio transmitter operator (RTO) will set up, what's our rally point should we be counterattacked, etc. Additionally, it's best that every soldier knows the plan which means it has to be communicated. Are you going to have a foot runner, or will all communication be radio or hand signals?

Continuing the reverse planning sequence, we would then ask: What do you have to know/do in order to place your automatic weapons? I would need to already have decided the fields of fire. To do that, I would need to understand the terrain the enemy is most likely to use as avenues of approach. This means the gunners must be informed of where to go on the hilltop once they arrive. They must be shown on the map, which means I need to get a map. Every man should be instructed on what he is to do once we establish a hasty defense on the hilltop.

Before we can set up our defenses on the hilltop, we have to first take it. The last thing we do prior to saying we have taken the hill is to "sweep through the objective," i.e., chase the bastards out completely. Before we can chase them out, we have to be on the hill. To get to the hill, I have to decide routes, assign squad duties, and field artillery (if available) must be timed with my movement. On and on, the reverse planning sequence goes.

With the business, sawhorse, and cake-baking example, you can see how easy it is to use this sequence. Before the customer pays the invoice, he/she must be satisfied with the product. To be satisfied with the product, I will need to prove its worth. I can demonstrate its worthiness by testing the product under the specific conditions the customer has requested. To test the product, I need to have one made and shipped to the testing location. To ship it there, I have to know the address, etc.

Brilliant! I thought, *absolute genius!* This reverse planning sequence is failsafe, foolproof. It is theoretically pure, and the only possible problems come from the execution of the plan. Then you can reverse plan some of those contingencies. What if the first squad gets dropped at the bottom of the wrong hill? What if the test prototype arrives damaged? What if my saw becomes too dull, or my oven doesn't heat as it should? Of course, you can't imagine every contingency, but you can **minimize the potential of chaos by planning backwards and communicating that plan to everyone.**

What about life? How might reverse planning affect your life? If you were to apply the reverse planning sequence and assuming you have a bucket list, what would happen if you were to apply the reverse planning sequence? What would you need in order to fill that bucket? Would you need to see Paris? Jump from an airplane? Live to see your children draw Social Security? Make peace with the Creator and believe you have been the best role model you could have been based on your personal circumstances? Identify them. Start there.

The reverse planning sequence is powerful within the US Army, among program managers (certified or not!), while writing computer code, and for living in general.

I thank CPT Phillips for telling me about it, but I know that in order to teach me, he had to read about it, and in order for him to read about it, someone else had to write it…

Reverse Planning. Go buy Steven Covey's book, and always begin with the end in mind.

Thanks CPT Phillips.

Chapter 8

Map Reading

I imagine some people believe there is nothing they can learn from the US Army, much less anything good. If you dismiss all of my previous stories as not relevant to you, then read this one. It definitely has the best chance of moving you into the group of believers.

The Army requires officers to be excellent map readers. We endured weeks of instruction on how to read a map, identify terrain features, communicate grid locations to others, measure crooked-line distances, read contour intervals, and learn the Army map symbols for the various types of units.

There is far more to map reading than just having a Rand McNally atlas. Not that those atlases aren't helpful, they most certainly are. They just assume there are details you don't need to know. For most Americans, an atlas will guide you from Atlanta to Omaha just fine. If you want to know more about what is in between those points, then you'll need a map with a closer, more detailed view than theirs.

Let's assume you want to communicate with another person about meeting at a lake by looking at a map. One of the first things you will have to do is make sure you agree on perspective. Are you both looking at a map of the same location made with a view from 10,000 meters above sea level, 25,000 meters, or 100,000? If you get the perspective wrong at step one, I guarantee that misunderstandings will ensue. A map with a 100,000-meter perspective is considerably different from a map with a 10,000-meter perspective.

Then, you have to be able to find the lake on the map. If there were only one lake in each of the fifty states, then it would be quite easy to locate, but if you live in Minnesota or Wisconsin, the precise location would be a critical piece of information. You can communicate which lake you mean in several different ways. You could say, "It's the lake ten miles north of Kenosha." If there's only one lake in that vicinity you will be fine, but what if there are two side by side and another on a farmer's property? Which do you mean? Of course, you could talk your way through that and ensure both of you are on the same page, but specifying a "grid coordinate" would be the precise method. The grids use the numbered longitude and latitude lines of the globe.

Atlases simplify that information by using their own letters and numbers. In some, the lines are drawn, others are not. With our example, put your finger on the bottom left corner of the map and move it to the right along the bottom, until you touch the line that runs closest to the left of the lake. Then slide your finger up that line to the last horizontal line below the lake. If there is only one lake then you could tell your friend: "I am talking about the lake in square twelveP." No confusion now is there? If you need to get closer than the size of the square, you can imagine ten vertical lines inside the twelve-P box and ten lines that run horizontally. Number the lines and tell your friend "Look at the lake at twelve, six, and P three." She would slide her finger to the sixth imaginary line from the left and then up three imaginary lines from the bottom of the P line. BINGO! Then you could both go jump in the same lake!

The next step is to determine where you are currently in relation to the lake and create a route to get there. Because each of you is in a different place, you can't follow the same directions to get there, even though the goal of getting to the lake is the same. Imagine telling your friend that to get to the lake she would do a left, left, right, left combination, the directions from your location. Imagine her arguing that "No, it's really a left, right, right combination, and if you don't follow my directions, you will certainly get lost."

See the parallel in life yet? Let me say it again: **Because each of you is in a different place, you can't follow the same directions to get to the same place.** She has to travel her route, you have to travel yours, but as long as you both agree on the final endpoint, it won't really matter.

It doesn't mean you have to plan alone, either, but you do have to do your own traveling. He can't make the trip for her, and she can't do it for him.

To be useful, maps require you know where you are. Understanding how you arrived at your current location is less important than knowing where you are going, unless you keep making mistakes that keep you in the same place. See any parallels about life here?

The only time you don't need a map? It's when you aren't moving, when you are idle, and you are content where you are. Maps can get you out of ruts or on your way to some place you believe is better than where you are currently. That means, however, you have to decide where you want to be first.

I admit that takes some soul searching. Maybe you want to become a certain kind of person, or want a job promotion, or want to live somewhere else. How are you going to get there? We know that you can't get to those new places by doing nothing or by doing the same thing you're doing right now.

Do you think this kind of planning takes away some of the romantic fun of just moving forward to see what happens? It might, sure. I guess it depends on how important the goal is to you. I find the prospect of success exciting, and planning for it is motivating! I assume most people want to be successful in their pursuits and prefer creating an environment that makes success more certain.

"Proper prior planning prevents piss poor performance," my commander used to say.

It's true.

Figure out where you want to go, who you want to become, and create a plan, then get going.

Chapter 9

Signing In

Branch insignia of the Signal Corps established in
1860 and original home of the U.S. Air Force.

Success so far! In May 1980, I was four years older, now twenty-one, a college graduate with a degree in history, had thrived in ROTC training, and left school in my blue '69 Mustang with a commission and set of orders to Fort Gordon just outside of Augusta, Georgia. Everything I owned could fit in that car, and I enjoyed the novelty of being a nomad free to go wherever I wanted, if I chose to. I had six weeks before my July 1ˢᵗ reporting date. I bounced around friends' homes, parents' homes, grandparents' homes, and attended a family reunion in Southern Illinois, all without really realizing my college-boy ways were not going to last forever. I left my Mustang with my parents and flew from O'Hare to Augusta.

Lessons from the Army wrap themselves around each other like intertwined, tangling vines. It's often difficult to separate them. Each lesson, however, like each vine, survives because of its own merit, its own truth.

I learned a good lesson during my first hour in the Army, before I'd even put on the uniform to report for duty the following morning.

I ran into a second lieutenant from the Puerto Rico National Guard signing in with Lt. Carpenter. He didn't have a place to stay that night. The only uniform I had was the Class A dress greens, but I didn't have the required black shoes! My colleague from Puerto Rico had fatigues AND a Class A uniform. I told him he could sleep on the couch in my Howard Johnson hotel room if I could wear his dress shoes for a day or two while he wore fatigues.

That's precisely what we did.

Luckily, his shoes fit, or they fit well enough. He slept and showered, and I wore his shoes until I got money to buy uniforms. (Officers were given a once-in-a-lifetime allowance of $100 to purchase uniforms.)

At the time, I didn't know there were lessons in that story, but like Moses in the cleft of the rock, looking back revealed its glory. A major lesson from that shoes-for-room deal is fundamental to the success of the Army. It's also foundational for coping in romance, work, finance, vacation, etc.: **Learn to make do with what you've got.**

General Eisenhower told the world that the ingenuity of the American soldier won WWII. I believe it. I've seen sergeants craft spectacular things with only the tools and materials at hand. I've seen food heated, doors built, cables made, and trucks repaired. None of them were done "by the book." Americans express that concept through the cliché "Play the cards you've been dealt." It's a great lesson in life, and the Army depends on it!

One can't learn this lesson by reading a book. You have to live through it to know how true it is.

Reduced to its lowest terms, this "making-the-best-of-what-life-gave-you" can be called survival. Counselors and psychologists advise that "sanity is doing the next thing." And insanity is continuing to do the same thing while expecting different results. In other words, if the cupboards are empty, sanity would be the drive to buy food. For me, sanity and survival that day in 1980 were exchanging a pair of black shoes for a free night at the Howard Johnson. I found a way to meet the requirement and survived my first day in uniform.

Survival is essential, but it may not be the only important lesson. I navigated that small problem and dodged a huge cultural and regulatory mistake according to US Army. I would have gotten nailed if I'd worn my dress greens with sneakers. I would have been chastised if I had shown up in civilian clothes. Instead, I forged a solution to my problem and saved my ass! As we know from Saint Augustine (though he never served in the US Army), he liked wine and women like a soldier: "An error in the beginning is an error indeed."

I avoided an error initially that could have labeled me for a long time "as that goofball who wore tennis shoes with his uniform." I survived my first full day because I had the desire to survive. I then thought of Uncle Phil back at the SAE house. Looking back on this room-for-shoes story, I had many options. I could have whined that somebody distracted me while packing my suitcase, and that's why I didn't have them. I could have moaned that my parents should have given me more money to buy a pair upon arrival at Fort Gordon. I could have told the Army they had to pay me so I could afford a pair of shoes, and it was really their fault and not mine. I could have also blamed my ROTC for not making me buy more uniforms. I know now what Uncle Phil meant. Those excuses would have kept me a boy.

"Make you a man" meant accepting responsibility, taking ownership of one's lot in life and its outcome. That day at Fort Gordon, the man inside me came alive and spoke: "You've got an issue, it's yours alone, you caused it, how are you going to handle it?" The lessons don't end there.

Chapter 10

Personal Affairs

During our first days in the Signal Officer's Basic Course (SOBC), the officer student company commander gathered us in the auditorium of Signal Towers. There, we filled out numerous forms while he explained the in-processing, the importance of keeping the last copy of your orders, and how to create medical files. He also outlined the expectations for future officers.

Except for the West Pointers, most of us were still in college-boy mode, sitting where we wanted, laughing and joking freely as if we were at a school assembly waiting for things to start.

During his briefing, the commander told us two things that have stayed with me.

1) Turn off notifications on personal electronics in public.

2) Keep your personal affairs in order.

The first one wasn't as important as the second, but it was still significant. He stressed that it was unprofessional for an instructor, or anyone, to speak to us while allowing our watches to beep. I find it rude today when adults or children play video games with sound in any public

Signal Tower before demolition

waiting area—restaurants, trains, planes, doctor's offices, etc.— (this was before cell phones) or have their ringer volumes set to max. Texting in public with the typing clicks enabled, talking on speakerphone, and making others listen to the videos they're watching is as rude as burping. Respect others. "Don't be rude," the captain said.

This era marked the introduction of watches sold with alarms and reminders. People believed they had status if they owned a beeping watch, which served as a reminder of some event known only to the owner and created a public nuisance for those within earshot. Those who needed reminders signaled their importance and purpose. Today, watches no longer beep because technology has shifted that annoyance to cell phones. In 1980, it was watches; today, it's cell phones.

I'd go one step further and say it is unrefined to have a cell phone conversation in public, period. Frankly, I don't want to listen to a casual discussion about Aunt Nelly's rose beetles or whether someone will car-pool to the soccer tournament next week. It's just plain rude. Have you ever been out to eat and forced to hear another diner talk (and no one whispers on a cell phone) out loud? What would they do if I started singing "The Star-Spangled Banner"? Uncle Sam told us not to be that public offender, and we turned off our watches.

You won't catch me with a cell phone with its ringer on at a conference or anywhere else that would inconvenience a neighbor. People appreciate that, and I bet they appreciate it about you, too. It's patriotic to decrease noise pollution!

Where I work, one fella gets called by his wife five or six times daily. His ringer is loud. "You have an incoming call, You have an incoming call…" (He wants to be able to hear it if he is at the end of the hallway). Another colleague's ringtone identifies when his wife calls: it's the sound of a fighting cat. It's funny; we all chuckled about it…the first time. Now I would rather hear fingernails on a chalkboard.

One lieutenant didn't turn off his watch, and the captain confiscated it, in front of everybody, only to give it to him later in private. He was serious. Yes, that captain told us to turn off our watch alarms and to be professional. I wish there were more Americans in that auditorium with us that day. From watch alarms, he turned to personal affairs, and I perked up when the commander told us to "Keep your personal affairs in order, all the time."

At twenty-one, I was surprised to hear that. I figured there was Army life and my private/personal life, like parting my hair down the middle. What he told us didn't align with my expectations. It seemed he was suggesting that our private life could impact our Army life as leaders.

Curious, I paid attention as he explained further. "Officers are expected to keep their personal affairs in order. This means paying your bills on time, settling pay problems, not bouncing checks, and taking time to go to the dentist, the doctor, the barber, everything."

Hmmmm, I thought. I was intrigued. He continued: "If you don't care for these things, they don't go away. When they don't go away, they become bigger problems. When they become bigger problems, then they will control your time."

"For example," he went on, "you ignored a slight toothache for several months, and now you have to go to the dentist because the pain is too severe, and your unit is supposed to deploy tomorrow. Had you done what you should have, you would have avoided this kind of problem. Now the unit is without an officer, just because you didn't want to bother with a personal problem when it first arose."

I never thought of it that way. I used to believe it was heroic to defer those responsibilities and demonstrate you were willing to prioritize the team over yourself. That's not how the Army, at least this commander, viewed it. He told us that you put the Army first by taking care of the Army asset, which is you, first.

Now, this isn't to be confused with other principles. Officers don't eat until soldiers have been fed. In this instance, you put the needs of others ahead of your own. Officers stand in the back of the chow line, especially when out in the field. At sick call, however, officers move to the front of the line, ahead of the enlisted soldiers who end up waiting most of the morning. See how this works?

It's for the benefit of the Army that officers let the enlisted eat first; when there's a shortage of food, it's the officer who is to go hungry. We called it "taking care of the troops." In the medical example, the Army needs the higher-paid soldier to return to work before the lower-paid soldier. Usually, officers (not always lieutenants) get paid more than the enlisted.

The commander's advice was solid. When I haven't followed his advice, trouble has found me.

Fast forward to Charlie Company at Coleman Barracks. West Germany in 1982. I was appointed to Company Executive Officer (XO), outranked only by CPT Tyler, the Company Commander. CPT Tyler, an OCS officer, had risen through the ranks and enjoyed leading the company in formation. We never ran less than two miles, and usually ran three to three and a half miles daily. Coleman Barracks, once a Luftwaffe airfield, sits three miles from the Rhine River. For months, our first sergeant and company commander kept saying we would run to the Rhein, six miles round trip, something we had never done before.

Running six miles is a long distance, but running in formation feels even longer. The idea loomed over the company like an ominous cloud—unreachable yet ever-present. We knew the location of the Rhine and the distance involved, but many lacked the confidence to complete it. It became the topic of conversation within the company, and with no definitive date in sight, the mystery cloud continued to hover over Charlie Company.

CPT Tyler and First Sergeant Ignacio kept the promise alive, building the fear factor in many and setting the "Oh Shit" response into motion. You'd hear soldiers say: "Hell, I ain't running that far. I've got a vehicle, and no Russian soldier will run six miles to catch me anyway!" Or someone would say: "CPT Tyler's just bucking for promotion, that's all." Stories of that sort abounded. It was the talk around the company area.

I began experiencing a problem with my left foot. Walking became painful. I ignored both the pain and the company commander's advice at Fort Gordon. Eventually, the discomfort became significant enough that I had to see a podiatrist, twenty miles away, in Heidelberg. There, he diagnosed me with "multiple mosaic verruca," another way of saying plantar warts all over my foot. He shaved them off, provided me with a solution to soak my foot in, and advised me not to wear a combat boot on that foot or run until I returned for a checkup. I was on restriction. The military jargon for such a doctor's order is: "He's on profile." Army officers dislike profiles because they believe they hinder performance and limit promotions.

After I visited the infirmary on Tuesday, the doctor placed me "on profile." At the end-of-workday formation, the first sergeant announced Charlie Company would "Run to the Rhine!" on Friday. The next morning, soldiers saw me wearing a combat boot on my right foot and a sneaker on my left. SGT Cappa asked me if I had gotten a profile to get out of running to the Rhine. I laughed and said, "No, I would rather run than have this pain." The mistrust he expressed, however slight or subtle it might have been, was now present and discussed among soldiers because I had a tennis shoe on my left foot.

Friday morning came, and I showed up ready to run to the Rhine. A few reminded me that I didn't have to run because of my profile. I said, "Yes, I do. How's it going to look? We've been talking about running to the river for two months, doing the buildup, and now the senior lieutenant has a foot profile. I have to run."

If I had listened to my first commander, I would have gone to sick call earlier and taken care of myself, the Army asset, but I didn't. I did what I thought was best, and what I thought was best wasn't.

Ever do that yourself?

I could have gotten in trouble for "violating my profile," ignoring the doctor's orders, and running when I was told not to. The usual rule in the Army is "if you violate your profile, it cancels the profile;" you don't get to claim "doctor's orders" and go back "on profile" because it's convenient. Can you see the pickle I put myself in by neglecting my personal affairs?

I ran to the Rhine that morning and didn't fall out or quit. I made it back and put my combat boots on again that same day. And you know what? Instead of soldiers talking about me intentionally getting a profile to get out of the run, they now thought I was hardcore for running despite my painful foot.

I don't know what it was, maybe it was pride or a sense of pride that said my body is above medical science, "I don't need no stinkin' doctors." Pride led me away from what needed to be done, allowing me to rationalize that my actions were best. That's how pride, the great deceiver, works.

No wonder theologians refer to pride as the sin most hated by God. The Old Testament and the New Testament alike, for both Jew and Gentile, pride is the favored sin of Satan. Hindus tell us pride only hurts the proud man, and Buddhists tell us pride keeps us stuck inside the revolving door.

Oh Yeah. My pride put me in that pickle.

If I could do it all over, I would have listened to that company commander at Ft. Gordon, and not delayed going to the doctor, and kept a small problem from creating a significant problem.

Chapter 11

Social Change Class of 1980

The Army created unique opportunities for me to witness historical events firsthand, events that would shape US history. Fortunately, my first assignment was just that. For some, it was a minor event, but for at least half of American society, it became a "tide has been turned" moment, a battle of Midway, a high-water mark.

Let me explain. The Army personnel system classified every officer by their year of commissioning. I was a member of "Year Group '80," commissioned on graduation day, May 18, 1980. The Army ordered me to the Signal Officer Basic Course (SOBC) 7-80, the July class. All the graduates from the US Military Academy at West Point assigned to the Signal Corps attended that same July class.

Just another July in another year doesn't sound historic. It was. For the first time, in 1976, the US Army allowed 119 women, two of them

Black, to enter West Point as cadets. It's a four-year school. 1980 was my year group; their year group was the first ever to have female "grads."

Previously, women served in the Women's Army Corps (WAC), which disbanded in 1978 while my future SOBC classmates and I were in school. In 1979, there were 8,890 female officers. In 1980, there were over 10,000 female officers, and by 1983, there were 15,000.[1] To give some perspective and provide context, I've lifted some text from the preface in Morden's history of the WAC:

> Many of the ideas and moral attitudes that existed in the middle decades of this century will seem strange to modern readers, but they lived and they influenced policies affecting the WACs. For example, until 1971 the Corps did not accept the initial enlistment of a married woman. Society expected that a woman would stay at home with her husband. Also until that year the Corps would not even consider enlisting a woman who had had an illegitimate pregnancy, whether or not a child was delivered from that pregnancy. Until the late 1960s most WAC detachment commanders did not allow enlisted women to wear blue jeans or slacks outside the unit area unless the women were en route to the softball field or bowling alley. A WAC in uniform could not enter a liquor store or a bar, smoke while walking, or chew gum in public. The rules were strict and were sometimes disobeyed, but the

---

1 http://www.army.mil/cmh-pg/books/wac/Chapter 13.htm#p2 Chapter 13, page 379
The Women's Army Corps, 1945-1978, Bettie J. Morden Center of Military History, United States Army, Washington, D. C., 2000

women learned high standards of deportment, and they knew their officers and NCOs cared about them as individuals as well as members of the Corps. By the late 1970s, society had taken such a wide turn in attitudes toward unwed mothers, unmarried couples living together, dress codes, conduct in public, and other standards that the strict morality and social proprieties of earlier years faded from existence.[2]

That America is gone today, and it makes me wonder why anyone would want to return to it, but that's what was normal in 1976.

As a young lad, I had always admired West Point and would have liked to go there: tuition was free, and cadets were paid 50 percent of what a second lieutenant earns. It's a good education; rather, it's an excellent education. Why didn't I? You don't get to go to one of the military academies just because you want to. One has to be invited, "granted an appointment." Who grants appointments? The President, the Vice President, US Senators, and US Members of Congress (MOC). Each MOC can have up to five students from their district enrolled at one time. Students who compete for this nomination are high school athletes in the top 5 percent of their class, with a clean record and all that entails. I lettered in tennis and maintained mediocre grades that I didn't really care about. I was not Academy material, and my family certainly had no inside political pull that often helps an applicant. They are great kids! If you ever doubt the future of America or suspect it's "all going to pot," then take a drive to West Point (or Annapolis). You will see your

---

2 Ibid, p ix-x, http://www.army.mil/cmh-pg/books/wac/

tax dollars being spent wisely and will walk away knowing America's future is in good hands.

I had only gone to college, not an academy, paid my own tuition, signed up for ROTC, and now was in a class of distinction with the first female graduates from West Point. Not that the distinction was mine in the slightest, but I was there, side by side with the first women ever commissioned into the Signal Corps by West Point. The fact wasn't lost on me, although we rarely thought about it then. I enjoyed talking to the female officers and listening to their stories of extra things they had to endure that men did not.

I'm not suggesting those four years were more difficult for the women; I can't. I bet they were, but I wasn't there. I can only say it was different. I can certainly say it wasn't any easier for the women than for the men. The year groups before 1980 hated the idea of women at the Academy, let alone in the Army (the idea is even questioned by some in the President's cabinet today), so the female cadets likely faced more harassment due to that attitude. Not one woman I know was bitter about her experience.

For the most part, their male peers accepted their presence without too may qualms. The USMA class of 1980 set the tone for the rest of the Army, demonstrating that female officers are competent, trustworthy, and forever part of the Academy system.

And you know what? The Army did fine.

It's an interesting thesis, and not the purpose of this book. Still, it illustrates a recurring lesson about the US Army, one few Americans, especially anti-military Americans, would care to consider. **The US Army has been a major contributor to social change in America.**

The US Army accepted Black people before the Civil War. It was the US Army that ran the Freedmen's Bureau, trying to ensure White America treated Black people fairly after slavery ended. Local peasants killed some White officers for siding with the newly Freedmen in different states. Proudly, several of the White officers charged with running the Freedmen's Bureau were from my former home state, Illinois.

The US Army successfully integrated Black troops ("colored" was the term back then) into units with White troops starting in 1949. No other organization in America could have integrated its ranks as peacefully. Left to civilians, the push for integration in Little Rock, Birmingham, Selma, and, more recently, in Boston shamed America.

The US Army advised against dropping the atomic bomb on Japan. Surprised to learn that? At a May 31, 1945, Interim Committee discussion of the atomic bomb, scientist and Manhattan Project administrator Arthur Compton was present. He recalled, "General Marshall stated that from the point of view of the postwar safety of the nation, he would have to argue against the use of the bomb in World War II…." Soldiers value life, and clearly, General Marshall expressed that sentiment in his opinion.

Now, in 1980, it was the US Army making the acceptance of female officers, White and Black, from West Point part of the American tradition. That same year group included the first Black Cadet Brigade Commander at the Academy, Vincent Brooks. If you remember the Iraq War coverage, he was the Brigadier General who gave daily briefings on television.

Yes, with its tradition and well-known insistence on putting values before self, the US Army has been an agent for social progress in America.

I am glad I met many West Pointers, "ring knockers" (they all wore class rings). There were a few arrogant ones, but only a few. The rest were fun and gave insights that a "ROTC" like me appreciated. Some of them only wanted to associate with other "Pointy Heads," but plenty of others liked stepping beyond the familiar faces. I've lost touch with them all, so if anyone knows a Ruth (Ellie) Griffin, a Mike or Donna Newell, Steve Tobin, "Mund," Kathy Wheeless, John Mazucca, or Tim Staggs from that historic class of 1980, tell them their name is in my book and I hope all is well with them.

If you search "females West Point 1980," you'll also find a YouTube video of my friend Ellie Griffin. She earned a PhD in Geology and retired in Colorado.

Women at West Point, Class of 1980

Chapter 12

It's Only Hair

As a history major at Westminster, a liberal arts college in Fulton, MO, the Army appointed me as an officer in the Signal Corps, the technical branch, without having taken a single course in engineering. The Army gives its future officers five branches to rank as a wish list. Since I was a kid, having seen the movie *Patton*, I always wanted to be an armor officer, tanks. Then I experienced what an infantry unit can do to a tank when the infantry is concealed. No thanks. Two of the choices had to be combat arms, which I made the fourth and fifth choices. At the time, the Signal Corps was the largest branch in the Army, and as my third choice, I was sure that was where I would be assigned. My first choices were Finance and Transportation, just as a joke, mainly because we all knew none of us were going to get those assignments. The Army's needs come first. They have experience in making music majors (BG Norman

1956-2001 (left) and 2004-Current (right)

Archibald) and history majors, like me, into Signal Officers. My first orders sent me to Fort Gordon, home of the Signal Corps, Augusta, Georgia, in the Deep South near the South Carolina state line. I didn't know much about Georgia, but I was aware that its state flag, adopted in 1956, included a rebel battle flag following the Supreme Court's ruling that separate but equal schools for Black people were illegal.

While in high school and college, I parted my hair down the middle. In the 1970s, when the era of Led Zeppelin, the Rolling Stones, and the Grateful Dead was in full swing, my circle of friends did the same. On the practical side, I also sported prescription glasses that darkened outdoors and lightened inside, sparing me the expense of owning two different pairs of glasses. I also happened to like grape soda and iced tea on occasion. In the Chicago suburbs, we teenagers always drank unsweetened iced tea. All day long. I didn't think anything of it. When there was a choice of soft drinks, I chose grape soda. Those had been my preferences for at least five years. No one during my officer training mentioned anything about what I like to drink to me, and I reported for Army duty as myself, with my hairstyle, glasses, and beverage preferences when beer wasn't an option.

At age twenty-one, this Yankee, whose great-great-grandfather fought at Shiloh and marched with Sherman through Georgia, arrived in July 1980 to begin the SOBC at a fort named after a former enslaver, white supremacist, and probable head of the Georgia KKK, Major General John B. Gordon. That July, I was overweight, had my hair parted down the middle, and was as clueless as any young man could be. I flew out of Chicago on a cool summer day, wearing corduroy pants and a long-sleeved shirt, and took a taxi from Bush Field in Augusta to the Howard Johnson's hotel where I had a reservation. In just a few minutes, I was sweating nonstop in the 90-degree heat and sultry humidity for which the South is well-known.

At the age of twenty-one, in the first months of my military career, I thought the Army was something I could compartmentalize. The rest of America does it. "Work is work, home is home, and I don't bring work home." "What I do in my free time is on me, and not my employer's concern." I assumed I could have a professional Army life, a private life as an individual, and never the twain would meet. I believed those things, but Uncle Sam doesn't work that way. Eventually, I learned and accepted that you couldn't be one way in your private life, and then turn around and be something different in your Army life. They are the same.

The cabbie drove me to Fort Gordon, where I officially signed in to the Army at the Officer Student Company. Second Lieutenant Carpenter, a red-headed kid from somewhere, himself a newbie to the Army, signed me in. I'm not sure he recognized the significance that signing in would have on my life and future, but I knew. I didn't know precisely, but I knew it was something significant. I felt it. For me, it was an event. For him, I was just another green neophyte borrowing his pen to sign the roster, but I knew differently. It's probably why I remember his name. I knew that I had just formalized the adventure I had promised myself to pursue. It was official; I was in the world's greatest Army. I showed up for duty on time, a feat in itself. I wasn't AWOL, not tardy, I met all expectations, and my military career was off to a successful start!

Regarding military preparedness, though, I wasn't ready when I showed up for the Basic Course. I understood that being fit was important; I could pass the PT Test to enter Ranger School, but by the Army height and weight standards, I was overweight. At seventy-two inches, I should not have weighed more than 195 pounds, but I did.

Nobody likes a fat signal officer. Our TAC officer, First Lieutenant Paul Albertelli, an Academy graduate, did the right thing and put me on the "fat boy" program. I don't remember what TAC stood for, but they were graduates of SOBC who had just completed a 3-year tour as a Signal officer assigned to be advisers to us newbies. I lost the weight, just as I was supposed to. I knew being overweight wasn't tolerated in the Army; I expected that and dealt with it (some more of that lesson from Uncle Phil). There was one reality, however, that caught me by surprise: a stereotype.

First Lieutenant Albertelli had just completed his first three-year duty assignment as a Signal Officer with the 25th Infantry Division in Hawaii. Lean, athletic, and shorter than most of us, he was our advisor and helped guide us through this introduction to the Army, setting a great example.

During a break between classes, he pulled me aside to tell me that in the Army, there is a stereotype. "Look, I'm sorry, I know this isn't fair, I know it's just a thing, but there's a stereotype in the Army that if you part your hair down the middle, and if you wear sunglasses, and definitely if you drink grape soda, then you are a doper. I'm not going to order you to change your hairstyle, but you need to know that's out there, and it's strongly accepted as truth, everywhere." I was shocked!

I had just completed four years at a liberal arts college, majoring in history, full of American idealism. I didn't quite grasp what he was telling me. After all, it was no longer the '70s, Vietnam ended five years ago, and protests had faded. That troubled generation of the late 60s and early 70s had run out of steam, and now it was our turn. I was in the company of educated people who were patriotic and motivated. To hear that the Army would automatically think of me as a "doper" because of my hairstyle was just preposterous!

"Oh, come on," I said. "You've got to be kidding!"

"Yep, fair or not, that's the way it is," he said.

With my liberal arts education, I immediately went into the Socratic method of discourse. I logically removed any solid foundation that suggested everyone who parts their hair down the middle is a doper. He listened. "I know, it's not accurate It's a stereotype, a generalization, but it's there."

For me, this became, in my youthful quest for truth and justice, a matter of principle. I could take on the culture of the US Army, and by my sheer competence as an officer, along with my intelligence, and willingness to work, I would be THE officer who parted his hair down the middle, and was well thought of. I would begin disassembling that stereotype, and the first step of that crusade started at Fort Gordon in July of 1980.

I checked it out with my peers. Most of them said, "What's the big deal? Change your hair!" Of course, I thought they didn't pick up on the clear importance of this gross injustice. I called my father, a former signal officer, and he didn't know there was a significant violation of principle involved, observing that "it's only hair." I decided then to make it my private rebellion. I wouldn't call attention to it, and decided I would be known by my deeds and strength of character, rather than by how I parted my hair!

Lieutenant Albertelli warned me, but I didn't listen.

I finished training and I showed up to my first duty assignment in January 1981 as a Platoon Leader in the 97th Signal Battalion at Coleman Barracks, West Germany. For those unfamiliar with military organizations, a battalion is comprised of four companies, and a company contains four platoons plus a headquarters (HQ) section. My platoon, larger than usual, consisted of fifty-five soldiers. Under Army guidance, leaders are responsible for everything their soldiers do or fail to do. It is the platoon leader's job to ensure soldiers get paid on time, are clothed, fed, trained, their families supported, and work assignments completed, especially the paperwork side of soldiering, promotions, school applications, efficiency reports, shot records, and PT tests—all of it. I showed up with my hair parted down the middle and my prescription eyeglasses that darkened in the sunlight. My sponsor walked me to Battalion HQ, introduced me to the staff, then returned to his duty. I met the battalion executive officer (XO), a major, and he asked me point-blank: "Are YOU wearing sunglasses?" (which was forbidden when in uniform or not on flight status). I said, "No, Sir, they haven't adjusted to being indoors yet." He reminded me that officers do not wear sunglasses in uniform, especially indoors.

An hour or so later, my unit sponsor, First Lieutenant Anderson, caught up with me and told me they (battalion leadership) didn't like my hair parted down the middle. "Oh Goddamn!" I said. I then mentioned it to my Platoon Sergeant, SFC Lutz, who had been with the Special Forces most of his career. His advice: "I know, Sir. My dad parted his hair down the middle for his entire life. It doesn't necessarily mean anything, but it is perception."

Face-to-face with a generalization I knew was inaccurate, and the complex reality that the stereotype would hurt me, I relented and combed my hair over to the side. I ditched the tinting eyeglasses and from then on wore only the miniature Buddy Holly-style glasses the Army issued. (They were called SMFM glasses, short for See Me, F* Me, because they were chick-repellents).

I learned several things, and one of them angered me: in every stereotype, there is a kernel of truth. That's how they get started. Someone doesn't just make it up; women like shoes, for example, or men will watch anything on TV that has a ball in it. We <u>know</u> not every woman likes shoes, and some men don't follow sports. The generalization isn't 100 percent accurate, but it's more true than not, and it ticked me off, because mostly, not always, that stereotype was true. Most of the people I knew who smoked dope parted their hair down the middle and liked grape soda.

I went to high school in a southwest suburb of Chicago. Most of my friends smoked dope. Everyone I knew who parted their hair down the middle, and many who didn't, were dopers. Some of them liked grape soda, and almost all of them liked iced tea. Many were the first to jump on the new bandwagon and got an ear pierced. Such was the environment that defined the context of my transition from high school/college boy to the US Army.

I was mad that the stereotype was predictably true and the Army could be right even without specific evidence. Their experience said: "If someone parts their hair down the middle, then they also smoke dope."

To this day, my idealism, my sense of what is fair, troubles me. My little voice tells me to stand up against every inaccuracy, but not every perceived injustice must be fought. I oftentimes need to be reminded of my father's words: "**It's only hair.**"

There will be times when great principles are at stake, and to relent would be wrong, but those times come rarely, and now I pick my battles wisely.

That winter day in 1981 was the last time I ever wore my hair parted down the middle; Mother Nature and DNA settled the future for me; now there is nothing left to part! Wouldn't that have been comically ironic, to continue to wage my campaign against the stereotype, endure the severe consequences, part my hair down the middle, and end up bald anyway?

Thanks, Lieutenant Albertelli.

Chapter 13

SFC Lutz and the Broom

The Army stateside is a different Army overseas. How so? Besides the obvious geographical considerations, the Department of Defense assigns every unit and organization a Force Activity Designator (FAD) of I-V. This designation tells the supply system which units to support first. FAD I units are already in combat. During peacetime, the military still designates the Special Forces, Delta Force, the SEAL teams, etc., as FAD I units. FAD II units are already positioned for combat, and FAD III units are positioned for deployment to combat. [I do not know if this FAD designator is still in use today, but they'll always have something like it.]

During the Cold War, West Germany bordered communist East Germany and Czechoslovakia, both Soviet Union assets. US foreign policy since Truman had focused on "the containment of communism."

This "bad thing" took root in Russia in 1917, giving us the Eastern bloc of communist nations, communist China, and, closer to home, the island nation of Cuba. The Vietnam War was fought in support of preventing communist North Vietnam from taking over South Vietnam. A significant goal of communist nations was to spread communism by defeating democracy. In the 1950s a "Red Scare" took hold of the country, and paranoid congressmen accused the government of being full of "commies." To their credit, there were communists in the government—and still are—but none have advocated overthrowing our government, or they'd be in prison. To this day, Americans often use the word "communist" as a synonym for dictator or fascist government, rather than using it in reference to an economic theory. When I want to have fun with friends or acquaintances my age and they say something I disagree with, I'll refer to them as "a commie." (They know I do not believe they are communists).

That was the context of my time in uniform. Stateside training focused on fighting the Soviet Union. We were not allowed to say "the Soviet Union" or "Russia" while discussing combat training; however, the Army ordered us to use the generic term "the Threat," and that's how we trained. We all understood what it meant, though.

The greatest probability of going to war during this Cold War, against the Threat (always started by them), would be in Europe with their attack through the "Fulda Gap" into West Germany. The Gap was two mostly flat land approaches into West Germany around a set of 2,000-foot mountains/hills (the Vogelsberg). Tanks move fastest on flat land. Because of "the Threat," almost every unit in Germany was designated as a FAD II unit. Most of the units stateside were designated as FAD III, ready to be deployed to combat. In Germany, we were already there for combat; we didn't have to fly or take a ship to engage the enemy. That is the significant difference between duty stateside and duty in Germany (or Korea). It is not a coincidence that the first units to get the M-1 Abrams tank and the AH-64 Apache attack helicopter were units assigned to defend the Fulda Gap. As a Midwestern, Protestant, I was leaving a FAD IV training unit in Georgia for a FAD II unit in West Germany.

Born in Illinois, I grew up primarily in Kentucky, Indiana, and Virginia, with three years spent in Germany, and high school in Illinois. My parents' family all hail from Illinois, south of I-70 near Saint Louis. Grandad Stahlman was a union carpenter, and Grandpa Bryan was a union factory worker, perhaps a machinist. Both were blue-collar, strong union employees. My mother was one of fourteen children. Her parents were born in 1894 and 1898, and my father's in 1904 and 1907. I grew up valuing work, doing things for yourself, figuring things out, and then helping others. Around my uncles and my cousins, I learned how to fix things, particularly my '69 Mustang. My cousin Ernie and I replaced its differential, rebuilt brakes, and bled the lines. I replaced the water pump (outside in January), rebuilt the carburetor, performed my tune-ups, and changed my oil, among other maintenance tasks. I had wheel ramps, a hydraulic jack, and jack stands. Additionally, because I had worked with Grandad, I had my own cross-cut and rip saws, hammers, and a drill press. I always traveled with a quart of oil, a gallon of water, wrenches, screwdrivers, and tape, just in case I broke down. (And a funnel. Funnels make pouring anti-freeze, gas, etc., much easier.) After high school, I worked as a janitor at Edwards Hospital in Naperville. During college, I poured concrete and worked at the Cerro Copper factory in East St. Louis (Sauget) in the summer. My cousins Don and Terry also worked there. I had working-class roots, but went to college among mostly wealthy White kids.

I brought that work ethic with me to the Army. After being assigned to 1st Platoon, C Co., I wanted to assure soldiers that their idealistic lieutenant was not afraid of work. I was committed to participating in any assigned burden, and I considered all of us a team contributing to our Cold War mission of defending NATO.

My Platoon Sergeant, Raymond Lutz, had been Special Forces with the 10th group in Bad Tölz, and also in Vietnam as an adviser. One day, the office floor needed to be swept. SFC Lutz was elsewhere, so I grabbed the broom and dustpan and started sweeping. Besides cleaning latrines, what lower work could have been done? I proudly showed that I was not afraid of doing menial tasks when needed. A couple of minutes into sweeping, SFC Lutz came running into the office and took the broom from me. He handed it to another soldier, told them to finish sweeping, and took me outside.

"Sir, officers do not sweep floors!"

"Well, I don't want soldiers thinking I'm afraid of work, SFC Lutz."

"Listen to me, sir, I was outside the company when SGT Ryan came over to me and said, 'Hey, SFC Lutz, your lieutenant is sweeping the office!'" Everyone who heard him must have had a good laugh at my expense over it. Inadvertently, well-intentioned, I naively added to the reputation of second lieutenants being stupid.

I relented. Okay, I made an error in judgment and took responsibility for it. Fortunately, SFC Lutz remained faithful to the "good order and well-being" of the Army by looking out for me and correcting me.

The lesson is not so much about not sweeping or doing tasks below one's status, but rather in recognizing that **just because you have rank and privilege doesn't mean you know everything**. The worst supervisors I ever had were afraid to admit what they didn't know.

Humility is a wonderful lesson and I learned it that day. Thanks SFC Lutz!

SFC Lutz fulfilled his goal of becoming a Command Sergeant Major and returned to Montana.

Chapter 14

Tomorrow

There are arguments about the best way to live.

First, you have to define what the word "best" means. For some, "best" means the most fun. "The best life is the fun life" is their motto. They make a good case. What fun is there in not having fun? Not much. You can make a life out of having fun. However, you have to define what fun is.

Generally, people perceive fun as the fulfillment of desires for laughter, smiles, and a lack of obligations, requirements, and responsibilities. Children approach life this way, while adults, particularly parents, show them that fun is valuable, but it isn't the reason for our existence. We can go out drinking and thinking that we got it made. We can ignore paying bills and spend our money instead on a cruise, a road trip, or a night out at the bar. Experience teaches adults, however, that this pursuit of short-term satisfaction can lead to long-term problems, such as sitting in a cold, dark house because paying the electric bill wasn't prioritized. Living solely for fun overlooks planning, making you a pinball in the machine called life. Before long, all you can do is react, ultimately you're unable to influence events.

Others define the best life as one without troubles, problems, tragedies, reversals—whatever name you want to give to adversities. They also make a compelling argument. Indeed, a life filled with tribulation cannot be considered the best life. Indeed, a life that keeps us in grief and sadness is less appealing than one full of joy. How can you avoid tragedies? You can't, but you can minimize their likelihood. We know that driving when you've been consuming alcohol increases the chances of something bad happening... to someone. We understand not paying bills on time can lead to financial issues, especially when money is owed to the IRS. Neglecting the maintenance of your car (or relationships) can result in swift disasters. However, you can prepare for these situations. You can arrange for a designated driver and set up savings accounts to cover year-end or quarterly tax bills. You can keep your car well-maintained to prevent blowouts or failing ball joints. You can also pay attention to your spouse.

You could also go overboard and spend most of your hours planning how to prevent imagined, but improbable, tragedies. Such a person would not be fun to live with either, no matter how safe their world is—living the planned life with the pursuit of safety as the greatest good leaves little room for spontaneous joy.

I learned a method from a fellow lieutenant who was also a platoon leader in Charlie Company.

Jim Duffy was a few years older. When you're twenty-two, someone who is twenty-seven seems much more mature. The Army was my first job after college. Jim had been a schoolteacher in Maine (like Colonel Chamberlain in the film Gettysburg), he was married with kids, and had that steady, unflappable temperament one expects from people in Maine. That put him way up on the maturity scale compared to me. I was still single and mostly worried about what I would do on a Friday night, where I would go, and how I would get back home. He worried about his wife, their home, and their children.

I was still a good lieutenant despite my youthful inexperience. My platoon sergeant was probably around thirty-six years old. If Jim seemed old to me, then how do you think a man who had been in the Army since I was five, jumped out of more airplanes than the number of mess hall lines I stood in, and wore a combat patch on his right shoulder appeared to me? I wasn't scared of him; I just knew he knew more than I did. He ran the platoon, but I was the platoon leader.

I recall speaking with Jim, Lieutenant Duffy, and telling him that I just couldn't get ahead of the game. That my time was being "overcome by events" and I was spending my time reacting instead of influencing or directing.

He asked me if I knew what my platoon sergeant was going to do tomorrow. I just looked at him, puzzled. I must have had that same look that German Shepherds do, cocking their heads at an angle. Curious. I said "no." He then said words that to just a casual observer, wouldn't have much weight, but they did me.

In the Army, you are expected to do what is expected of you. You are expected to set examples, to have answers, and to know how to solve problems. As a leader, you are responsible for setting direction, defining the vision and goals, and moving the group towards that end. Jim's words, though positive, carried with them a scolding without the tone of harshness. For an officer not to do something he should be doing is the same as being ineffective. It's not a good thing to be inefficient. The officer's review system is even named "OER" the Officer Efficiency Report.

I answered Jim that no, I don't know what my platoon sergeant is going to do tomorrow. Without pausing or emotion, he looked at me and said: "You should."

Great advice, yet again. This time it came from a peer, albeit an older and wiser peer. I incorporated it and soon began the habit of meeting with my platoon sergeant at the end of the day to discuss the next day's events before we left the company area that night. It took some time. Things didn't fall into place immediately, but soon I began to be proactive, no longer reactive. Soon, I was influencing the day's events and leaving the pinball role to others who hadn't planned their time.

That practice has served me well. The best brokerage firm in the nation, Edward Jones, which was also once my employer, required us, the new salesmen, to have the next day's call list prepared the night before, making us promise to never put our heads on our pillows without first planning the next day. You can do this with your children, friends, parents, and, most importantly, your spouse. When both of you discuss hopes and dreams for the coming day, you will wake up together to face what's ahead. You'll have a head start on the day! You don't have to spend the morning discussing and defining. You can go out and live!

Plan your next day. It simplifies life, reduces the likelihood of arguments and troubles, and ultimately leads to more fun.

Thanks, Lieutenant James Duffy, wherever you are.

Update: Jim retired at the rank of Colonel.

Chapter 15

Choosing Friends

Company C, "Charlie Company," was the "get up and go" company of the 97th Signal Battalion in 1982. Our NATO mission was to install mobile radio relay systems across Germany as an interface point between other nations' armies. Within the battalion, Charlie Company was the first to deploy and the last to come home. The other three companies in the battalion couldn't function until we completed our mission. Everything hinged on us.

To explain this, consider your home. Charlie Company would be what is behind the wall jack and the connectivity to the rest of the world. The items you plug into that telephone jack, fax machines, telephones, etc., represent the other companies of the 97th. As the radio relay company, we deployed radios carried inside shelters on two and a half ton trucks and set up the antennas. It was similar to cell towers of today, except we took ours back down, moved them, and set them up again on other hilltops. Until our radio systems were operational, the pressure and spotlight were on C Co. Once established, the pressure shifted to the telephone and message center companies, until we relocated. Then it started all over again. If Charlie Company failed, the entire battalion failed.

In 1982, the senior non-commissioned officers (NCOs), battalion commander, and S-3 (operations officers) came to us straight from the 82nd Airborne Division or Special Forces Group. They brought that culture to Germany with them. They recognized that C Co. was a potential single point of failure, so the battalion commander put his best officers and NCOs in Charlie Company. Within Charlie Company, we held that to be true, without any doubt. Charlie Company spent at least one week per month in the field, more than any other company in the battalion. We were the first to deploy, the last to come home, and we took pride in that mission. We had the toughest assignment in the battalion and believed we were more important than the other three companies. We also exercised more than they did. We ate C-rations more often, ran longer distances in formation, lived outside longer, and our soldiers got into more fights than theirs, frequently in downtown Mannheim in the Turkish bar, Alcazar, soon to be marked off-limits to US personnel. Charlie Company was the roughest company in the battalion and carried that reputation throughout the entire post, where infantry, cavalry, and aviation units were stationed. We worked hard and played hard.

Considerably larger than an infantry company, C Company, with 240 soldiers, had over 120 vehicles and generators, plus four platoons of fifty-five soldiers and an HQ section. B Company next door had ninety soldiers, a platoon and a half, and we mocked them by referring to them

Former headquarters and barracks of C Company, with B Company behind it.
Coleman Barracks, Sandhofen, Germany.

as "B-Platoon," akin to calling a soldier a Boy Scout. We thought B Co. did little more than sit around waiting for us to finish our work, then worked for a day or two and called it quits. They worked and were good at what they did, but we enjoyed the rivalry, like siblings picking fights with each other.

One night at the Officer's Club, we started taunting the officers of B Company. I was friends with those officers and held nothing against them; we were in the same Army but still hassled each other.

"I heard B-Platoon was going to be absorbed by Charlie Company."

"Yeah, well, the only reason you guys spend so much time in the field is that you need the practice!"

It didn't take very much to set off our short-fused Senior Lieutenant Danby, who had served as an enlisted man in C company. One insult

Officers Club BFV Mannheim, W. Germany today, (now closed)

too many, and he lunged across the table at a B Company officer. I stood up, ready to throw in. I don't remember any counter-punches thrown; somehow, it ended quickly. He and I got the hell out of there as fighting in the Officer's Club wasn't considered appropriate conduct, and I wasn't going to stick around to watch someone point the finger at me, especially when I knew the MPs were coming. We regrouped outside, and I remember feeling, perhaps even expressing, that I would back Lieutenant Danby anywhere, any time. I had found something greater than myself and belonged to it. Charlie Company wasn't just a job; it was now an identity. The MPs walked past us, up the steps into the Officer's Club, and we drove away.

Looking back, it was silly. Bravo Company and Charlie Company were on the same team. Together, we hated Russians and communists, but here we fought each other simply because we could, which is an example of a tendency men have I suspect wives hate, but is the part of men that women need at times, our strength. We protect. Feminists can sneer at the bravado and machismo that flowed that night, but perhaps this is the part they hate most: we thought it was fun.

Did I think our senior lieutenant reacted inappropriately? I do now, but he was my operations officer. He just wasn't as quick-witted as that lieutenant in B Company, but he was agile and athletic. He jumped and reached across that table for the guy, and I thought to myself, *Oh Shit, here we go*! Staying seated and telling Lieutenant Danby to calm down, explaining that B Company was just jealous for spending their overseas tour doing half of what we did wasn't an option. No, if I wanted to be a part of this company, I had to make a split-second decision. I chose to side with Lieutenant Danby, right or wrong, and I did.

Fortunately, it de-escalated quickly; I didn't want to start my Army career with a referral from the Military Police. I knew people observe how you conduct yourself under stressful situations and form conclusions about you. (They sized me up with my hair parted in the middle.) It's all part of building a reputation. In his book, *The 7 Habits of Highly Effective People*, Stephen Covey tells us that if your preferred method of problem-solving is a hammer, you tend to see everything as a nail. I didn't want to be that kind of leader; I wanted my troops and my superiors to see me as solid, stable, and reliable.

On the other hand, I wanted to show enthusiasm and loyalty for Charlie Company. I wanted that more than I liked the idea of ignoring the insult or calming Lieutenant Danby down, so I stood up, ready to start throwing punches and shoving bodies. Had I remained seated, stayed out of it, and merely watched events unfold, that timidity too would have had repercussions. "You didn't back me up," or "You were too scared." Call it immature, I was twenty-two, I could live more easily with a fight on my record than to work for the next three years with the reputation of timidity.

That's dangerous thinking. It's necessary at times, but it is risky. Luckily, it's not needed as often as we might like pretending it is.

The primary lesson here is to be careful about who you follow. Being loyal is generally good, but it's not the most important thing. The Nürnberg trials at the end of WWII taught us that following orders, because that is your lot, your role, doesn't excuse your actions when following illegal orders.

That skirmish in the Mannheim Officer's Club wasn't very immoral or illegal. It was a clue, however. Did I want to be like Lieutenant Danby?

You have to follow, but you don't have to imitate. I would gladly do what Lieutenant Danby told me to do, but I didn't want to imitate him or be like him, even though he was an overall good guy, and I liked him and respected him for coming up through the ranks.

Most of us, at least those of my age and older, recognize this lesson. It's the youth, and I was twenty-two then, who do not. You can tell a lot about a man by the company he keeps, and eventually, **bad company will ruin good character**. Lieutenant Danby wasn't bad company; I just wanted a different role model.

Do I regret standing up, willing to fight alongside Lieutenant Danby? Nope, not at all. I am glad things turned out the way they did, but had they turned out differently, I would have regretted it. That's the rub. You don't know how it will turn out once you start something. I was glad, still am, that I didn't end up in the stockade that evening. I was also pleased that there was little mention of the scuffle around the battalion the following week.

I lucked out. I threw in with someone I didn't know much about, and that outcome was a roll of the dice. The lesson? **Choose your friends wisely**!

By the way, Lieutenant Danby was promoted to Captain and appointed Company Commander of, you guessed it, B Platoon!

Chapter 16

SP4 Johnson

The field artillery claims to be the King of Battle while the infantry declares itself the Queen. Each branch boasts its prowess. For the Signal Corps, its "braggin' rights" come from the words of Five-Star General Omar Bradley in his book *A Soldier's Story*: "Congress can make a general, but it takes communications to make him a commander." In other words, the artillery king is useless if the infantry queen can't tell the king where to put it. Much like the three rules of real estate investing— "Location, Location, Location"—the Army has three maxims: "shoot, move, communicate."

The infantry would do the shooting, everybody would do the moving, and the Signal Corps would handle the communicating. What good is it if the infantry captures a town but can't tell anyone they've done so?

Communication is a fundamental skill, and the Army has deemed it extremely important. During the Cold War, doctrinal training taught us that communications were considered "target number 1A" for our potential enemies, "the Threat" (the US Army's politically correct term for the Soviet Union). Our nuclear capabilities were their target number one. First, they wanted to stop us from launching atomic attacks, and then they aimed to prevent us from communicating with each other.

Sounds smart to me, doesn't it to you? Did you notice our priority of targets during the First Gulf War? Our most important targets were the enemy's air defense system and their communications. An inability to communicate hobbles a modern army, forcing it to rely on foot or motor messenger service. Every military commander knows this whether they're good guys or bad guys. Communication is important. That is true without question, but communicating excellently is difficult.

As far as I can tell, communication has at least three elements. First, there must be a physical link between two points. In other words, a listener has to be able to hear the speaker. We cannot communicate if you are in St. Louis watching the Cardinals at Busch Stadium while I am at home watching the game on television. Cell phones make that physical connection possible, and once I dial correctly, we can communicate from my house to your stadium seat. Establishing that physical link across the battlefield is the mission of the Signal Corps.

Secondly, once the talking starts, you have to agree on what language to use, and then the variations in vocabulary such as sizes, slang, etc., within the chosen language.

Once that gets settled, then the emotional element must be considered. The third element includes feelings, tone of voice, enthusiasm, and intent. Intent. Capitalized. Feelings are the filter, the prism that bends the speaker's intent. "That's not what I meant!" Ever said that to a loved one, or had it said to you? This third level is where I have had the most trouble, and it's here where the Army taught me one of its great lessons.

I was a platoon leader of the 1st Radio Relay platoon. As such, I had an assigned jeep and driver. One time, while on maneuvers, I returned to the rear area to retrieve some critical equipment that was urgently needed. Specialist 4th Class (SP4) Johnson was my driver. We drove the twenty miles from our hilltop and arrived at the rear area. I told him I would go to the Electronic Maintenance shop and arrange to pick up the equipment. That's all I told him.

That was my mistake.

Within an hour, I completed my tasks and returned to my jeep, where no Specialist Johnson was to be found. I looked around the company area for him. Not in the mess hall. Not in the day room. No one knew where he was. Maybe he walked to the snack bar to get a hot meal. I checked there.

No Johnson. Maybe he needed to exchange dollars for German Marks at the American Exchange. I walked there, no Johnson. Perhaps he went to the maintenance shop looking for me. I looked there. Specialist Johnson wasn't anywhere to be found on Coleman Barracks.

About an hour and a half later, he showed up at the jeep. Perturbed, I asked, "Where the hell have you been, Johnson?" He told me, "Sir, you said you were going to take care of those things you needed to do, so I went home to my wife and

Ford M151a2 like my jeep, Charlie-100

did a load of laundry." I looked at him, ticked off. Pausing, I replayed our departing conversation in my mind, realizing that I had never told him when to return to the jeep. I assumed we were on the same page, that he too was concerned about what I was worried about. I looked at him sternly and said, "OK, Johnson, this one's on me…"

Did he take advantage of a new lieutenant and play me so he could go home and see his wife while the washing machine ran? You bet he did. He had me, and he knew it. If I had told him not to leave a post, he would not have gone home. If I had told him I would only be there for an hour and he could take the jeep to the snack bar, and I would meet him there, he would have done that. I was vague in my communication, and it was general enough to protect his actions.

I thought about making an issue of it further, because he wasn't dense. We were on a mission, and we both knew it. However, the company first sergeant and the company commander would have told me it wasn't a big deal, that "he burned you. Now learn from it, and move on, lieutenant." So I moved on and learned my lesson. Here it is:

Don't communicate to be understood; rather, communicate so you are not misunderstood. It was a damn good lesson, and it has served me well whenever I recall it.

The lesson from the interaction between Johnson and me doesn't end there. I try not to be sexist, but I am male. I am biased with the male view of the world and life. I really can't apologize for it either, but I can acknowledge it. I have heard women, more than men, express astonishment when their man doesn't "just know" what she thinks he should know, or what she meant, simply because he loves her. Mistakenly, she might view his inability to read non-verbal communication as a symbol of the entire relationship. On the other hand, he listens to her words, and not her tone, or subtle messages, and therefore misses a lot.

Of course, I realize this is a stereotype, not unlike my hair parted down the middle story. However, stereotypes are formed around there being some kernel of truth somewhere!

The Army can even help couples. Men, imagine your wife as the commander, and you are required to listen for her intent, just as the Army taught you to anticipate your commander's deci-

Lt. Stahlman on some hilltop in W. Germany, 1982

sions. Ladies, men don't like being required to "pick up on clues." Your girlfriends are good at that; men are not. It doesn't mean your man loves you less if he doesn't come to the same conclusion you do just because you would like him to. Ladies, pretend your man is Specialist Johnson, be clear and direct, and I'll wager romance will flourish!

Speaking clearly to avoid misunderstanding offers numerous positive benefits in the workplace. Many times, even recently, I have expressed a single thought only to see senior management twist that statement into something unimaginable! Communicating effectively to prevent misunderstandings is a crucial responsibility. If you neglect to make sure you're communicating to avoid being misunderstood, life will be even more challenging than it already is. It reminds me of that bumper sticker: Life is Difficult. Imagine what it's like if you are stupid too.

I liked Specialist Johnson. He was a good soldier, and he taught me a lesson. I hope he and his wife remember that afternoon fondly.

Chapter 17

Ass Chewing

I eventually made the transition from ROTC cadet to Army officer. However, this transition wasn't complete during my time in SOBC, and certainly not while attending the Radio Systems Officer Course, where the workday allowed just as much free time for studying as it did for class. As a student in these courses, I never got my ass chewed until I went to a unit.

The first ass chewing came as a surprise. It happened during my assignment as a platoon leader in the 97th Signal Battalion, Mannheim, West Germany. I showed up at Coleman Barracks, and luckily, the battalion commander assigned me to Charlie Company, the radio relay company. We spent more time in the field than any other company in the battalion, always the first to deploy and the last to return home.

The other companies, A and B, couldn't do squat until we achieved our objectives. We even deployed weeks in advance of the infantry or the cavalry (who think there is no Army outside their missions). Our company spent a minimum of one week per month in the field. Note that I said minimum. Charlie Company always spent the last few weeks in August and the entire month of September in the field, weeks before the infantry showed up to practice their skills. Then we went right back out in October and November. I recall talking to a senior warrant officer, saying something like: "I'll be glad after this requirement is over." He said: "Why, we're just gonna turn around and do something else." I laughed. Yes, that was just the way it was.

I was still a second lieutenant, and everyone expected me to be stupid. They call it "stupid," but it's not stupid; it's a lack of experience in both the Army and life. During my first "field problem," my platoon had to run about a mile and a half of cable from one location to another. The cable segments come in ¼-mile lengths and require a repeater every fourth segment. We used a piece of test equipment called a PTM-7 to test the cable segments. The soldiers who ran the cable earned the Military Occupational Specialty designator of thirty-six Charlies (36C), but we called them "cable dogs." They had the most physically demanding job, as the quarter-mile reel of PCM cable (CX-11230) was extremely heavy, and laying cable had strict rules. It's supposed to be eighteen feet above the ground, or it has to be trenched and buried to avoid being damaged. (The Signal Corps hates tankers and artillery because they like to drive across our cables and make us work even more.) In addition to that, the steel fibers in the cable poked through the shielding and could easily cut your hands. Being a cable dog wasn't rocket science, and this specialty did not attract the brightest in the Signal Corps, but I liked them because they got things done.

CPT Frank, the company commander, West Point class of 1974, came out to my cable run and told me how to use the PTM-7 to test the cable properly. He specifically showed me how to attach the cable to one port on the box and clearly said: "Your cable NCO will want to connect it this way," as he changed the cables to demonstrate it. "I don't care what he says, this is wrong, tell him to do it this way," as he configured the cables to other ports on the PTM-7. I nodded, "Roger that, sir!"

I called my cable section chief, Sergeant Ai, and told him the captain wanted the segments tested with the PTM-7. Enthused, he hooked up the PTM-7 just like the captain said he would. I told him not to test it that way, and he said: "Sir, in school this is how we were taught, I've always done it this way, and what you're saying isn't going to give you an accurate reading on this cable segment."

Sergeant Ai had been in the Army for about five years. I'd been in the Army for about seven months. He worked with cable more than CPT Frank did, certainly more than I did, and a little voice told me to "show your subordinates you trust their expertise, lieutenant." We tested the cable as Sergeant Ai wanted it tested.

I reported to operations that the cable mission was completed. Soon thereafter, I was informed that the communication over the cable wasn't working. CPT Frank drove back to my location to investigate. "Did you test the cable segments with the PTM-7 Lieutenant?"

"Yes, sir, we sure did."

"Did you hook it up the way I showed you?"

"No, sir, Sergeant Ai said that was incorrect, and we tested it the way he knew how."

"Goddammit, Lieutenant. I told you how to test it." Angry, CPT Frank re-cabled the PTM-7 as he had shown me, and sure enough, that cable segment failed the cable test and those cables could not be used.

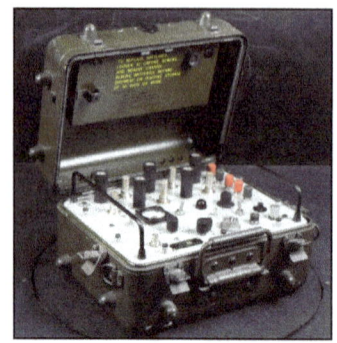

AN/PTM-7

"Get another reel of cable out here and test it the way I showed you the first time, and don't let your subordinates dissuade you when you've been told the correct way. You've learned a lesson tonight, now get this link up and running."

There was no time for discussion. It wasn't academic. He said his piece, jumped into his jeep, and took off for his next destination.

I imagine the ass chewing had to happen. If I had told Sergeant Ai that his method was wrong, that his five years of experience and schooling would be overruled by a second lieutenant younger than him and with barely as many months in service as he had in years, he would have resented me, especially if I was correct. Sergeant Ai stood there and watched CPT Frank pull me aside to "coach me."

I reckon I could have passed the ass chewing on to Sergeant Ai, but that didn't fit. I made the mistake; it was mine, not his.

I learned quite a few lessons from this. Central to succeeding at work is the familiar adage: **if you think the boss is wrong, he's still the boss**. We get paid to do what the boss thinks is best. I also learned not to give carte blanche trust to subordinates or others just because they have been doing something for a long time. I let Sergeant Ai talk me out of doing what I knew should have been done.

In the longer view of things, I got my butt chewed, but Sergeant Ai knew that I would listen to my subordinates, and that I was willing to shield them from the heat from the higher-ups when it came. I stopped the buck right there. I don't know if Sergeant Ai ever appreciated my ass chewing, and I never pointed out his involvement in it, but you can bet we never again used the PTM-7 any other way than how CPT Frank showed us.

Chapter 18

The Tower

Many people prefer learning through experience, by doing. Most soldiers are that way, which distinguishes them from the officer corps. The NCOs liked to think of us as book-smart "college boys" lacking in practical knowledge, especially us junior officers. For them, it was a point of pride to make such remarks. Much of that was really about the age difference.

When I came on active duty, the first sergeant and all the platoon sergeants were older than me, and more worldly. I knew that, accepted it, and felt on occasion that I should even refer to the battalion sergeant major as "sir," something for which he would have rightly rebuked me. "Don't call me 'Sir,' I work for a living."

They were older, not always wiser, but certainly knew the Army far better than I did, and probably far better than I ever would. They could teach me about day-to-day, hands-on experience. Like most junior officers, I had learned only from books, specifically history books. I welcomed their lessons, but they rarely enjoyed hearing about what I'd learned in books.

Two "book lessons" have remained with me forever, and they came from a biography of Douglas MacArthur, *American Caesar*, by William Manchester.

Before email and the internet, the inbox was a physical tray that sat on a commander's desk, labeled Inbox. Some had an Inbox, Hold, and an Outbox. MacArthur used only an Inbox and an Outbox.

MacArthur developed the habit of never going home with anything in his Inbox and didn't believe in a Hold box. I didn't think such a great thing could be so simple: "How to never get behind is to choose never to get behind." The way he did it, while a young commander, was to never go home with something in his Inbox.

I had trouble with it as a young lieutenant, I was a young man with some issues with authority. Procrastination allowed me to get the job done, just not exactly on time. Of course, that immaturity didn't advance my cause, impress my commander, or reflect positively on me.

Then I read about General MacArthur, and I tried it. I couldn't believe something as simple as: "**Don't go home until your Inbox is empty**" could make that big of a difference. I had nothing to lose, so I decided to try it. I stopped going home when there was still paperwork in my Inbox at the end of the day. Then I started seeing the results. When the battalion's list of overdue efficiency reports came out, none of my soldiers were on it! I emptied my Inbox every day; it became a habit, and my name fell off that "Always Late on Paperwork" blacklist that the

Army has. It worked, and worked well! I stayed on top of requirements and eventually earned a reputation for dependability, all because I chose to keep my Inbox empty and never got behind.

Sometimes simple things have a significant impact. What things in your life might this be true for? Maybe eating one less piece of bread each day will change your physique, or perhaps one daily kiss for your spouse or a pat on the back for a child will have significant benefits. Who knows? I do know it worked with the Inbox, and I'm willing to bet that one small change in other areas of life can yield similar positive results!

The other lesson I learned from General MacArthur was one he learned from his father, Arthur MacArthur, himself a Lieutenant General in the US Army. His advice to his son: "**Never give an order that won't or can't be obeyed.**"

Seems simple enough, too, doesn't it?

Some who have never served in the military believe that all an officer or NCO has to do is bark an order and it gets done immediately, that everyone falls silent, and the world turns because Napoleon has spoken. You hear it today in the civilian world from some managers. "I don't care what they want; this is what they are going to do!" or "We don't need their input; we are the bosses, not them."

That works, but it's not much fun, is it? In the long run, it doesn't even work.

George Washington talked about the character of the American soldier, and the trait he observed still lives on 250 years later, fused in ourselves as some cultural DNA. Our first President said that American soldiers are different; they have to be told "why" when given an order. Less than one hundred years later, Arthur MacArthur gave his son similar advice.

Giving orders and having them obeyed solely because of rank is effective in basic training and military schools. In the real Army, orders have to be agreed upon, or at least they must seem somewhat plausible. When they aren't acceptable to the junior soldier, then the qualities of leadership must rise to the fore.

Soldiers, like people in general, don't like being told to do "stupid shit." If they are told to do that, they want to believe their actions fit into the overall scheme of their work. When your order fails the other person's test, you must set the example and demonstrate your willingness to participate in the required work.

It's not that soldiers will rebel. They are better than that. They'll do what they are told, but the leader has to decide what kind of unit he is going to build. I've always wanted a team environment, not robotic automatons. When soldiers, people, know that you care about what's important to them, then it's a lot easier for them to follow your orders, and that's precisely what the Army wants.

General Arthur MacArthur knew this, and he wanted his son to know it too.

My father told me the story of a time when he was a platoon leader at Fort Huachuca and his unit was getting ready to go out in the field, but all of their preparation chores were interrupted because the commanding general wanted a pile of rocks moved off post to another location where a visiting dignitary wouldn't see them. The general would have been embarrassed if those rocks had been seen.

My father's platoon spent the entire day digging up rocks and throwing them on the back of the trucks, scratching the paint and getting them dirty. They wasted preparation time hauling rocks instead of completing all the necessary tasks for a deployment. My dad spent the day with his platoon and endured the seemingly stupid requirements of that day.

In the Signal Corps, we had to install radio and cable systems. Radios have antennas, and antennas need to be free from obstructions, like buildings, hills, and trees. This meant they had to be installed above the tree line. In Germany, the trees can be very tall, often reaching heights of seventy feet or more. Sometimes our antenna kits weren't capable of getting above the treetops, and we'd have to use towers built by other units. These towers were not permanent structures. They were pieces of hollow aluminum pipe assembled into a square to whatever height was needed to get the antenna above the treetops. Inside the square was a set of landings and stairs (no walls, so there was minimal wind resistance) that you could climb to the top.

Did I tell you I was afraid of heights? I had one site with a ninety-five-foot-high tower that needed to be used for mounting the antenna. My soldiers had to climb up there and do that work. CPT Frank told me, "Use the tower, and if your soldiers don't want to climb up because they are afraid, then you go up first."

I knew it. I knew I had to do it. Imagine if I had ordered that PFC up that tower to go alone while I stayed safely on the ground. Think he would have respected me more if I had done that? He could have told me he wasn't going to climb that stinkin' tower, and I couldn't have made him. Oh sure, I could have yelled, taken him back to the rear, and gotten him busted, but he still wouldn't have had to climb that tower.

We climbed that army green tower together, and I think they could tell I wasn't thrilled about it.

If you've ever pulled an antenna cable, you'll notice it gets heavier the higher it goes. We had to get the antenna cables up that tower, and you couldn't haul the heavy reels up ninety-five feet and then lower the

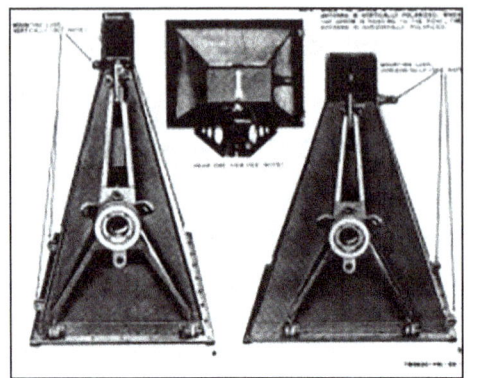

Bottom view of the thirty-inch antenna (left).
Not the actual tower. Ours was dark green and ninety feet tall.
This picture comes from HNA.de Alheimer Kaserne (right).

cables down. So, we dropped ropes, tied the ropes to the cable, leaned over the railing, and hoisted them up. The higher we pulled the cable, the heavier it became. Then, we had to do the same to get the antenna head up the tower, being careful not to bang it into the sides of the tower on its way up. My arms got a good workout!

We secured the antenna to the tower, attached the cable, and established the radio system. I didn't give an order that was going to be disobeyed, and doing so ended with a successful outcome. Lieutenant General MacArthur was able to give his son that great advice because he knew soldiers. His Army advice helped me, and now it can help you.

Chapter 19

No Excuse, Sir!

CPT Tyler earned his commission through Officer Candidate School (OCS), where he was selected from enlisted soldiers to attend the highly competitive program. He took command of Charlie Company and was then promoted to captain after completing his assignment as a general's aide. Before that, he also served in Charlie Company as a new lieutenant.

He was a stickler. He held everybody's feet to the fire, knew the ropes, and anyone who dared to bullshit him better duck, because he would fire back with both barrels. Most people don't like being held accountable, and we soldiers were no different. His insistence was never personal, and he saw his role not just as the commander, but also as training us lieutenants (there were five of us) to become solid officers and prepare us for increased responsibilities. Knowing that, we believed in his cause, and he earned our loyalty.

From him, I received the greatest compliment ever on my efficiency report. About me, he wrote: "Definitely not a 'Yes man.'" To this day, that is my most cherished description of my approach to work. He saw my personality not as a threat, as many supervisors have, he understood I was a young man committed to doing what's best.

Invariably, he'd find something wrong that happened within my platoon and make it my issue. It was constant, and you hated to see him coming your way. The other lieutenants and I nicknamed him "T." We'd run into each other around Coleman Barracks, and one of us would ask if we had "seen the old man?" "Yeah, T's on his way to battalion," and we'd purposely take a different route to minimize the chance of encountering him.

It didn't matter what was happening; there was always something else to improve. "Lieutenant Stahlman, how come your platoon is behind on submitting three efficiency reports (ER) for your NCOs (Non-Commissioned Officers, "sergeants")? I'd tell him what I thought was the answer:

"Yes, sir, the platoon sergeant told the section sergeants to get them done."

"Where are they? They're not here."

"Well, sir, the staff sergeants haven't met with the sergeants because we are still recovering from our return from the field." In my mind, I was telling him we had work to do that was more important than paperwork.

"They were due last week."

"Sir, we just got back from the field."

"Lieutenant Stahlman, I want those NCOERs turned into the company clerk, Brooks, so she can get them typed up and submitted to battalion by Friday."

"Yes, sir!"

I was part of 1st Platoon, while my peer, Jim Duffy, who was less senior but more experienced, led 2ⁿᵈ Platoon. Jim, too, went through OCS right out of Basic Training and was CPT Tyler's favorite lieutenant. We teased him a bit and referred to him as "Golden Boy." He didn't mind, and we weren't being vindictive about it.

One day I told Jim, "Man, CPT Tyler dogs me and I tell him the answer and he just keeps going on about it, refusing to see what I'm saying."

Jim said, "You wanna know how to stop that?"

I looked at him like he had some secret potion in his pocket he wanted to sell me, as if there were some magic I could conjure that would end these frustrations.

"When he tells you what's wrong and asks why, answer him with 'No excuse, sir.'"

He went on, "Once you tell him that, he knows you agree that something is wrong, and that you accept responsibility for it, which conveys you are going to fix it, and there's nothing more he can say. If you keep going without saying that, he's going to keep pressing until you accept it."

Brilliant!

"Lieutenant Stahlman, Electronic Maintenance scheduled service for your TRC-112 and told me it didn't get there."

"**No excuse sir**, I'll check into it and get that van over there right away."

That was it! It worked! The conversation ended, and he walked away happy, and so did I.

That's an excellent lesson for work. It helped me throughout my career, and if you've not adopted that method yet, give it a try. It's sure to end well if you do.

Chapter 20

To Soldier or Not

Before the arrival of LTC Clegg as our battalion commander, the 97th Signal Battalion didn't take soldiering all that seriously. Physical training was required, but the existing leadership would cancel it on a whim. If someone didn't feel like participating, they were told, "OK, you can sit this one out." We worked hard and played hard, but morale was lacking. Many NCOs would break out a case of beer after successfully establishing communications. It was a bit of a party, a fun-time approach. "Why can't we have beer if all of our stuff is good?" I had heard some say in their defense.

Drinking during lunch hour was permitted, too. Soldiers had the choice of eating in the battalion mess hall, going to the AAFES snack bar (the Wal-Mart of the military), or going to the Kantine managed by German contractors who sold Bratwurst, and Eichbaum Bier. I remember SFC Lutz while in formation saying: "You can drink NO MORE than two beers at lunch, and you cannot drink your lunch!" That changed with the arrival of LTC Clegg.

LTC Clegg was commissioned through the Ohio State ROTC program in 1965 and loved soldiering. He earned the green beret as a special forces soldier, the ranger tab, and served in the 82nd and 101st Airborne. During his time in Vietnam, he ran part of Company F, 51st Infantry, which was the Long-Range Patrol (LRP) teams in Vietnam working in Laos as part of "The Secret War." In addition to that, he was six foot four inches." We all thought of him as John Wayne.

His arrival at the 97th Signal Battalion may have been a letdown to him, as he wanted to command the 82nd Signal Battalion at Fort Bragg. There are more lieutenant colonels than Signal Battalions; competition for command slots is intense. As a result, our paths converged at Coleman Barracks in Mannheim, Germany.

His transformation of the 97th from a show-up, do your job, go-home type of unit, to soldiering seriously, where everything was urgent, could be studied as a how-to by MBAs at Harvard or Wharton Business School. The further away I get from that experience, the more I realize how radical and sweeping the changes were.

He called for a meeting with all officers in the library's meeting room, and we all saw him, up close, face-to-face. I was glad there were two ranks between me and him; captains and majors had to interact with him, not me. I stayed in the back of the room and heard him tell us: "I am firm, fair, and unforgiving." A silent intake of air, a quiet gasp, was felt by all. It was his warning order, his "I told you so when we first met" assurance of accountability. "This unit has work to do, and I'm going to see to it that you officers accept full responsibility for getting it done."

Was I going to become a man, or stay a boy? Was I going to stay a college frat boy, where everything is a joke, or was I going to soldier?

LTC Clegg, unable to command 82ⁿᵈ Sig, was able to pick several officers and senior NCOs from Delta Force, and the 82ⁿᵈ to help him. SFC Lutz was glad to see this new team arrive. They were his people. Similarly, though intimidated, I wanted this change too. I didn't want to complete my four-year obligation, leave, and have my time in the service to be just a continuation of "a good time." I wanted to soldier.

Soon, the order went out that whenever we salute or return a salute, we are to announce the battalion motto: "Tried and True!" I admit it felt silly to start doing that around Coleman Barracks, where we had a reputation for belittling such displays. Once we started, though, I liked it. It said to the other person, "This is my unit, of which I am proud. I am a serious soldier, and I believe in my unit's mission."

The expression "Can Do!" sounds rather trite to me, but LTC Clegg brought that attitude, and it was infectious. He was precisely the type of commander the nation deserved, and he was forging us into that vision.

In preparation for a major exercise, the Return of Forces to Germany, called ReForGer (FAD III units deploying from the States to practice combating the Threat in Germany), the Central Army Group NATO held budget meetings in Heidelberg. LTC Clegg was in attendance when the staff considered reducing the expense of porta-potties by not providing them to our battalion. LTC Clegg was not the whiny type. He didn't say "woe is me, this is so unfair" (although it was). He talked slowly and deliberately. His eyes could pierce, and his softness in tone reminds one of hearing Val Kilmer say, "I'm your huckleberry." He moved his big head in synch with his words, and he told those who outranked him in the room: "My soldiers will have porta-potties." It would have been easy for him to say, "OK, that's what HQ decided, nothing I can do about it." However, he was willing to face the blowback on behalf of his 800 soldiers. That's leadership.

A lieutenant friend of mine who had been in "B-Platoon", reassigned to HQ staff in Heidelberg, attended the meeting and relayed the story to me. I asked, "What happened next? How did it end?" He said, "Y'all got your porta-potties."

In a pre-deployment meeting with officers and NCOs, LTC Clegg told all of us: "Each soldier will have at least one hot meal a day while we are out in the field." For A and B companies, that was not too difficult a task. They were usually co-located with the brass, running switchboards and teletypes. Charlie Company was often alone. When we had to install radio links over forty miles, we had to deploy a three-person radio relay team. They were isolated, sitting on a hilltop out in the woods, away from civilization. Getting them a hot meal every day was going to be difficult.

One night, my then Platoon Sergeant, SFC Brooks, himself out of the 82nd, went to a relay site only to learn from the E-5 Team Chief that they had not received a hot meal that day.

I don't know why that happened. The sergeant said, "Sir, the colonel promised us a hot meal." I said, "OK, let's see what I can do." It was dark. We were not near a city. There was a small village about fifteen miles away. SFC Brooks said, "You know he's going to say something to the colonel about broken promises." I recognized that, and off we went to find a restaurant. I don't know how we found one. I was grateful I could speak German, and we ordered some "schnitzel sandwiches with fries." I was low on cash, SFC Brooks funded most of the purchase, and we delivered food to the team on the hilltop. The chow was hardly warm by the time we returned, but they got a meal that was not C-rations.

I don't know if that team chief was pissed off or glad that we were able to do that, but I chose to be faithful to the pledge our battalion commander made. SFC Brooks agreed. That night, I decided I wanted to be the best I could be, instead of slacking off on the sergeant and his crew, telling them, "Tomorrow is coming, we'll get you a hot one tomorrow, can you wait?" I understood what LTC Clegg was doing. He was building trust through promises made and expectations met, and I embraced his values. The Army, not just LTC Clegg, celebrates selfless service, and I was experiencing it and today I remain grateful for that opportunity.

Chapter 21

Influence What You Can

On my Officer Efficiency Report, LTC Clegg ranked me in the top three of the lieutenants in the battalion. Of course, I wanted to be number one; we all did, but none of us could outdo "Golden Boy." We accepted it, without hard feelings, without petty jealousy. I was pleased to be ranked that high. We all knew he put his best officers and best NCOs in Charlie Company. That alone said a lot.

I learned much under his command. One expression I picked up from him was: "He's the kind of person who talks about you as soon as you leave the room." I had never heard it worded that way, but we've all worked with and or been around, people like that. I call it being phony, and I don't respect people who act that way. I certainly don't like it when I catch myself doing it. LTC Clegg was a solid mentor.

He approved my appointment to be the Executive Officer under CPT Tyler after two years as a platoon leader in Charlie Company. That put me in charge of Company equipment readiness, as well as electronic and motor maintenance. I loved the motor pool and working with mechanics because theirs was a real-world mission daily, plus I used to work on my own cars, and I understood their language. The signal soldier doesn't get to practice their craft every day, setting up antennae and radio systems, but replacing axles and engine parts on vehicles and generators is a real challenge every time.

Since I no longer had a platoon, I wouldn't be traveling across Germany to check on things. I was now the Company Operations Officer, but LTC Clegg said: "No, Charlie Company, you don't get an operations officer in the field, Stahlman's going to be an Operations Officer in my battalion operations." The company commander didn't mind, because he knew, as one of his lieutenants, I could tell him what the battalion was thinking about overnight (as the junior officer on staff, I got the overnight shifts).

I don't fully remember the details; it may have been about trying to get another unit to agree to work on a circuit that was important to us, but not as important to them. As part of his briefing, I explained the situation with the circuit to the colonel, including the steps I had taken and the calls I had made. I told him I couldn't make any progress. It might not have been as important as I thought, but LTC Clegg thanked me for the information, looked directly at me, and said: "**Influence what you can, and let the rest go.**" I thought, *Holy Shit! That is profound*! I said, "Yes, Sir." And have never forgotten it. It ranks as probably the best bit of advice I've ever received, not just from the Army, but in life. I struggle with it still. I don't like giving up. When I know something is wrong, and

I know what ought to be done to correct the wrong, but it just will not happen, I have to accept that. I don't have to wail about the injustice. It does not mean I endorse it either, and from time to time, I will remind others of the issues.

It runs a bit counter to the words of the brilliant Winston Churchill, who urged people to be magnanimous in victory and defiant in defeat. I suspect what LTC Clegg meant was, don't beat yourself up over and over, don't keep running your head into that wall when you cannot influence events. To mistake the guidance as wisdom from Homer Simpson, "If at first you don't succeed, Oh Well!" is not the message either.

LTG Hal Moore was often quoted as saying, "Three strikes don't mean you're out, and there's always one more thing you can do to influence a situation towards your favor."

Sounds very similar to the Serenity Prayer.

God grant me the serenity.
To accept the things I cannot change;
courage to change the things I can;
And wisdom to know the difference.

LTC Clegg retired as a full Colonel and opened a family business in Florida. He's buried in Arlington National Cemetery.

Chapter 22

You're Indispensable

After my tour in Germany ended, I was reassigned to Fort Gordon, where I attended the six-month Signal Officer's Advanced Course. Leaving Germany was tough, not just because it was December and my wife was expecting, or because I had to get our car to the States, pick it up in Charleston, and find a suitable place for us to live in Augusta. It was hard to give up being a contributor, an "influencer." I knew the company's operations inside and out—technically, tactically, logistically, and most importantly, operationally. Being forced to leave, I knew the time had come. Part of me wanted to believe they couldn't do as well without me, so I considered volunteering to stay longer. This would allow us to get through the next Inspector General (I.G.) inspection, ensure the vehicles weren't deadlined, and maintain our readiness. It's a great lesson in the Army. You just might be "All that, and a bag of chips," but the Army will be fine without you. How does that make you feel? Sure, I made contributions. Soldiers (most) were glad I was their officer. That feeling of being indispensable creeps in, and of course, you want to believe it. However, the Army trains soldiers. It's not just the Army, the whole American military trains people so that each soldier can perform the job of the person below them and the person above them. The fancy term for it is called "continuity of operations," avoiding a single point of failure. Sure, losing a first sergeant or a commander is going to create chaos for a unit, but it's not a show stopper, unlike our Soviet counterparts who used to train such that almost every decision on the battlefield had to come from a higher up behind the line. (You can see evidence of that still in their ill-advised war against Ukraine, and in how their chain of command gets paid.) So saying goodbye and leaving is part of Army life. I envied the West Pointers in some regard, because they seemed to have most of that already drilled out of them. While I would reflect on saying goodbye, whether I'd ever see those folks again, believing I had made friends with many or several I'd stay in touch with forever. They just said: "See ya." Perhaps I'm just sensitive. So saying goodbye to Charlie Company challenged me somewhat, not that I ever considered not doing what I was told, but if you remember the old TV show M.A.S.H. when it comes time for Radar to return home to Iowa he's in "I am too indispensable to leave" mode. Hawkeye yells at him: "WE DON'T NEED YOU!" It's true. The Army needs somebody, but it doesn't have to be you. The Army's good for your ego and it's also good at keeping you humble. In my first civilian job where new employees were hired at a higher salary than my existing years of service, I eventually went to my boss Joe, a Navy veteran to talk with him about the requirements for a raise. (He was actually one of the best bosses I ever had).

He understood, but asked me if I had ever put my hand in a bucket of water and pulled it out?

"Of course."

"Well, that hole you left behind in that water is the impact of you leaving this $12 billion company."

The Army prepared me for that. The lesson here is more of an alarm, a warning. When you start thinking an organization needs you more than you need them, you're probably on a vanity trip. **Keep an honest appraisal of yourself.**

Chapter 23

Uniforms and Wives

This story comes from my experience in Germany and later in Washington, DC In Germany, the 97th held an Officer's Call regularly, maybe every other month, or a Hail and Farewell, where the officers and spouses welcomed the newcomers and said goodbye to those leaving. These were enjoyable social cookout gatherings. At one event I attended with my wife, we were talking with one of my favorite officers, CPT Wipperman. He was an Infantry Officer assigned to our battalion, working in his secondary MOS as a maintenance officer.

She and I were talking to him when I said, "CPT Wipperman, I came home one day and caught myself talking to her like I would talk to one of the troops. She sure didn't like it, and I sure didn't want to be that kind of husband."

He scolded me, "No, no, no, you can't do that, Lieutenant."

"I know, sir, but how do you do it—being infantry, more militarized than Signal?"

He said he and his wife developed an understanding: she gives him an hour to unwind from being around soldiers all day, and as soon as he walks through the door, he takes his uniform off!

"Aha!" I exclaimed, "Often, I'll leave my uniform on for hours after work, just because…"

He emphasized, "Don't do that—taking off the uniform gets you out of your role, your rank, your work mode much more quickly."

She liked the advice too and gladly offered an hour of grace, and I changed into my civvies as soon as possible. It worked. I don't remember ever talking to her like that again. The lesson here is, your spouse is not part of your work—take an hour, and make the transition to being with your family.

Wives and uniform stories don't end there. You can't just show up at work in the Army. Being there is only part of the requirement. To show up, you had to have already done a lot of work. Your uniforms had to be pressed, starched, boots shined, hair cut short, and mustache trimmed.

Sounds easy, doesn't it? Women have a tough routine every day with makeup, conditioner, blouses, hosiery (?), and so on. I quickly realized that having only three sets of uniforms and one pair of boots left me feeling stressed and busy every night. Sure, it was easy to shine the boots the night before; that was the case the first time. But then they'd get dirty during the workday. All that cleaning, polishing, and shining could be undone in just one workday, or even one hour. Even when they got dirty during the day, you had to clean them right away. You can't set an example by walking around with dried mud on your boots and expect other soldiers in the American Army to take you seriously when you tell them to clean their boots. It doesn't work that way.

Every night, I would go home, clean the boots, and then polish them again. It took about an hour's worth of work. Then I had to press the next day's uniform, which was generally two hours of additional work, assuming you had clean uniforms to iron. Otherwise, you had to launder them, which meant finding a washing machine and dryer. Luckily, my German Hausmeister provided one in the basement of our three-story apartment building.

I quickly discovered the on-post dry cleaning and began having my uniforms sent out for washing and pressing. That saved time, but I still needed enough uniforms to keep me going while one batch was being cleaned and pressed. It became a routine of baton passing. Turn in a dirty set, take home a clean one. As long as I could make it to their shop during business hours, things went well.

The same thing applies to boots. However, in Germany, there wasn't anyone willing to shine boots, unlike in a Korean assignment. That obligation was all mine. I kept three pairs of boots. One was shined to a high degree, one to an acceptable degree, and the other pair was just for being out in the field.

My time in the Army was probably when I owned the most pairs of shoes in my life, and it gave me a slight insight into women wanting shoes. (I still don't think I understand that, but all I have to do is accept it.) Having a pair ready for any occasion was a valuable lesson.

It's the same in the working world. Having tomorrow's clothes ready the night before is a time saver and a stress reducer. It's also your responsibility. You can't blame your wife for clothes not being prepared when you are the one who has to wear them the next day.

I recall one of my reliable senior NCOs complaining because his wife had put dark blue socks in his gym bag instead of the required black ones, which violated regulations. He was complaining about her, making his socks her fault.

"I told her what socks I needed!"

I corrected him, reminding him that he's in the Army and has Army feet, which require wearing Army socks. There's nothing in the regulations that makes it a wife's responsibility.

He quieted down, but I doubt he liked it. That ties back to the acceptance of being a man or remaining a boy.

If you know what you're going to wear to work in the morning and have it ready the night before, your mind can focus on other important things. It's a valuable lesson the Army taught me, one I often regret not following.

Update: that Sergeant's wife, Marian, who packed his dark blue socks, was killed in the Pentagon on 9/11/2001. He retired from the Army, and I hope he and their daughter are doing well.

Chapter 24

Major McDaniel

After completing the Signal Officer Advanced Course, I sought an assignment in the armored cavalry. I liked their mission and their bravado. The cavalry operates ahead of the Army divisions and functions as a "screening force," moving back and forth across the battlefield to locate or engage with enemy frontline soldiers. There's only one signal officer per maneuver battalion, and I wanted to understand what the rest of the Army was about. I told the assignments officer I would prefer being assigned to an armored cavalry unit. Still, she assigned me to a non-TOE unit (a non-battle organization) headquartered in the Pentagon in Washington, DC I didn't want to be a staff officer, "Boring!" but luckily I ended up in one of my most enjoyable assignments, Chief of the Air Traffic Control (ATC) division, at Davison Army Airfield, near Fort Belvoir, VA.

My office was on the third floor of the control tower. The tower was located across the runway from Davison Aviation Command, which was responsible for providing Priority Air Transport (PAT) for Department of Defense leadership in the Military District of Washington (MDW) and serving as the aviation assets for the 3rd US Infantry (The Old Guard) during presidential evacuations. They had a real-world daily mission, keeping me away from the paperwork piling up on desks in an office at the Pentagon. I loved knowing that what I did was important.

Despite having never been trained in ATC or rated as a pilot, I threw myself into the work. Although it took some time to learn the language, processes, and requirements, I performed well. The snack bar was on the other side of the airfield, and sometimes I would go there to engage with pilots from other airfields, introduce myself, and ask them how their approach went. In those days, the Class B uniform allowed no badges, ribbons, etc., so others never knew if I was a pilot or whether I belonged to the Aviation Branch or Signal Corps. My greatest compliments came from pilots who believed I was rated because I knew the subject so well.

Also across the airfield, just outside the snack bar, sat Major McDaniel's office and his #2 Chief Warrant Officer 4 (CW4-called "Chief") Preston. In those days, Warrant Officers (WO—called "Mister") were not allowed to lead troops. They possessed technical proficiency, and that was all the Army wanted them to do. Their expertise was indicated by the number in their rank. At that time, CW4 was the highest (they added CW5 soon after). As you can guess, most of them became pretty crusty by the time they reached CW4. They generally had no time for silliness (i.e., whatever they thought was silly) and enjoyed their stature at the top of their field. I never challenged a warrant officer,

View from helicopter #3 taken by me while participating in a ceremonial fly-over during the dedication of 'The Three Servicemen' statue in Washington, D.C., November 11, 1984.

certainly not a CW4, and any junior officer who would dare better be right because commanders almost always sided with the warrant officer. CW4 Preston was different. Oh, he was at the top of his field, no question about his competency, but he was approachable. I could engage him without him rolling his eyes at my questions. He reported directly to the Airfield Commander, Major McDaniel.

"Airfield Commander" does not mean the unit commander. Major McDaniel and CW4 Preston oversaw the physical airfield. That included runway condition, crossing lights, power, facilities, and ramps where aircraft are parked, and hangars. All of that was their responsibility. Major McDaniel had a giant whiteboard, six feet tall and five feet wide. On it were written all the projects he managed. There must have been twenty, far more than one person could reasonably manage, and his list of things to get done seemed to increase continually. In his way, CW4 Preston

The Tower at Davison Army Airfield, Fort Belvoir, VA. The third-story window was my office window. The Army has since built a new control tower, and when I worked there, the Army Aviation Brigade flew UH-1 Hueys.

used to scold Major McDaniel by trying to corral him to things important and urgent. "Sir, if you just complete one task each day, you'll get ahead of that list."

Ever feel overwhelmed? The air conditioning isn't working. You're out of milk and bread. The car needs tires, the kids need braces, and you're going on a business trip tomorrow. Mr. Preston's advice to Major McDaniel in 1984 is as valid today as it was then: **"Finish just one thing."** You'll feel better at bedtime, and waking up won't feel as burdensome. Mr. Preston's lessons didn't end there.

Major McDaniel's habits irritated Mr. Preston. He used to say things to the Major I would have never dared to say to a boss.

I pulled him to the side once and asked him, "Chief, how do you get away with talking like that to a Major?"

He said, and this is good, a lifelong lesson: "Sir, you can say anything you want, if you've got a smile on your face."

I snickered. I had never considered it. It's true, I tried it. **People respond to the feelings you communicate far more than the words you say.** For example, I once had a neighbor, just a few years older than me, who didn't care at all about how his yard looked. Now, I'm not so particular that a few taller blades of grass bother me, but I keep my yard fertilized and free of crab grass, dandelions, and leaves. My neighbor didn't care. His tree limbs drooped five feet above the grass, hung over his driveway, and the elephant grass was never trimmed; there were sticks everywhere, and I couldn't see the house next to him because his neglected overgrowth obstructed the view.

Annoyed, I ran into him outside once, and with a big smile on my face, like CW4 Preston, I asked, "When are you going to take care of this jungle, Buddy?"

He half smiled and said, "Yeah, I oughta get somebody out here to take care of things." It worked!

I lost touch with CW4 Preston. He retired from the Army and returned home to Alabama. I don't know anything about Major McDaniel. I hope his to-do list is small.

Chapter 25

DA Photo

The world has its rules; I've got mine.

I set the rules by which I live; I define what is important to me. An external source, like a carrot hung in front of my face, usually does not make me walk faster, work harder, or behave accordingly. I am my own commander—not any family member, not any friends, and certainly not any employer—unless I agree. Fortunately, I want good things: to be a decent father, a loyal friend, and a dependable coworker, but I'm not willing to give up my values to accommodate other people's plans.

Sound familiar? Then you've got the same problem I have: an issue with authority, a questioning of the rules just because they are the rules. There is always a better way of doing something, and certainly the "way we've always done it" is not, in my opinion, always the smartest, most efficient way of "doing it." Sometimes it is, however.

Does it cause you problems? It does for me. In the realm of Jungian psychology and personality temperament, I am known as an ENTJ, called "the Field Marshal" by authors David Kiersey and Marilyn Bates in their book on character and temperament types, *Please Understand Me.* (It and updated versions are available in bookstores.)

Other authors describe the ENTJ as the conceptor/knower. It's a fun test, and very often people who take it end up laughing out loud as they're reading words that describe themselves so accurately. In a nutshell, people are either Extroverted or Introverted. They prefer "winging things" intuitively, or they prefer processes (think of cooking without or with a recipe). They prefer feelings or facts when making decisions, and they either like things finished and complete, or "let's just wait and get some more information before we decide." I'm an extrovert, trust intuition more often, facts more than feelings, and prefer things to be settled. They also have to make sense and operate efficiently. I respect tradition, but when it hinders truth or efficiency, I feel little obligation to sustain it simply for its own sake. If maintaining the same methods you've always used is essential to you, then we are likely to have differing degrees of conflict.

In my theoretical, perhaps infantile, little world, everyone would see and agree with my reality. Those who don't simply aren't as committed to truth or efficiency as I am, in other words. However, I know I am not "all that." I'm smart enough to recognize that I don't know it all and am mature enough to accept other views (even if I believe they're wrong). I understand that everyone brings value to an organization. Do you have some of these reservations within you?

Test yourself... How many times have you stood in line at the Division of Motor Vehicles and thought that the way they make people wait to get their pictures, plates, and licenses is the most efficient method? How would you answer that? Aside from those who work there, I imagine the number of people who believe that is quite small.

There is one big BUT, however. They are the ones with the power, not me, not you. They have the rules on their side, the trump card. It matters not how brilliant you are, how right you are, how much more efficient your ideas could be. They have the muscle; you must play by their rules, or you don't get what you need. Either you get the license as instructed, or you don't get the license. Yes, No. Go, No-Go. There is no discussion. It's settled, over, case is closed. Stay a boy or become a man, once again.

So what did I learn from the Army about this kind of situation? The Army always wins.

The Army requires you to keep your personnel file up to date. I hated it. I wanted to tell them to go pound sand. I was a platoon leader in a TO&E deployable unit and was successful. I was a staff officer and successful, so go screw yourselves. You have my efficiency reports; get over it. That should be enough.

The Army, however, required a photograph. It was referred to as the "DA photo." You had to wear your Class A uniform "dress greens" with everything in its proper place: your pants correctly hemmed, your hands, facial expression, and every detail considered to determine whether you were suitable for future promotions and assignments. I hated it. I hated the idea that some REMF (Rear Echelon Mutha-F_ _ _ _ _) would think they could judge my character, intellect, and work ethic by looking at a picture of me and reading a page and a half written by my commander.

I tried to remember LTC Digh's advice that "It's only part of the game that's got to be played. Cooperate, graduate." I still hated it.

It was important, though, all of that bullcrap. Important, that is, if you wanted to be rewarded by the Army. If you wanted to be promoted, it was an absolute, nonnegotiable, fundamental requirement. In other words, without an updated photo and personnel file, I can guarantee you would not get promoted, and everyone wants a promotion, don't they? At least, that's what they tell you. Promotions meant more responsibility, which meant more money, which meant a proven track record of performance when you left the military and joined the civilian workforce.

It was all self-serving. I hated that. I hated that just being a good officer wasn't good enough. I hated being around people who wanted to "work the system" to maximize their advantage and profit from it. In some sense, David Stockman from the 1980s under Ronald Reagan was correct when he said (paraphrased): The majority of those in service care more about their retirement than they care about the work they do. Unfortunately, that's life in general.

Yep, I hated that part, but my disgust did not change that requirement. LTC Mann (who, in my opinion, should have never been promoted beyond Lieutenant Col) was insistent that I update my Department of the Army (DA) photo. HA HA. It became a contest for me to avoid updating it. Oh, I took the photo, but I never turned it in; I always found some flaw that would surely be pointed out by some reviewing officer, with power, whom I never met. Poor LTC Mann stayed on my ass about getting that pic taken, and I never did submit one after I was promoted to Captain.

The other reason I didn't take the picture was that I was already thinking about getting out of the Army and working for the CIA. I didn't want my picture to be available in a national database that might be seen by someone conducting background checks. I purely concocted this reason on my own, but I believed it.

The application for the CIA was a seven-page document. I got it from the wife of an employee who worked for the agency. She handed it to me at church, so that others would not, could not, say that they saw me talking privately with her CIA analyst husband. The instructions on the application told me not even to tell family members that I had the application. So, not taking that picture, when I was going to get out anyway, now seemed a wise decision.

But I didn't work for the CIA. In fact, I didn't even turn in the application. I took a civilian job in Boston instead, as the idea of leading a double life was more than I wanted.

The funny thing is, despite never having a picture of me on file as a captain, I got promoted to major in the Army Reserve. Take THAT, LTC Mann! I got promoted, and I didn't do it your way. Put that in your pipe and smoke it! Where there's a will, there's a way! More on that in a few pages.

The lesson here is that the world has its requirements. I can't change them; their rules are there for a reason. If I had been committed to staying in the Army for twenty years, I would have complied with that ridiculous DA photo and defended its requirement to guys like me. In a large organization, you can only advance your self-interest if you play by its rules. If you don't care about greedy self-advancement, then disregard it, but you have to ask yourself this question: Is not playing by the rules beneficial for you and your family? No, if I had stayed in the Army, I would have gone along with that DA photo and made sure they had all my assignments recorded correctly.

So that's the lesson. Keep your personnel file accurate. It will determine your future, which leads me to its crossover in the civilian world: your credit report.

For younger Americans, you have to stay on top of your credit report. (Now I sound like LTC Mann, don't I?) It determines what you are charged for car insurance, car loans, mortgages, homeowners insurance, and whether a company wants to hire you.

I hate it. I hate that some goofball corporation that has never even had lunch with me is going to assign me a three-digit number that the rest of the world is going to believe about my character and talents. Their formula for computing their score, called FICO, is a closely held secret. My griping doesn't change the world or how credit is scored. Complaining has never stopped the rain, the cold, or the snow, and it's not going to stop the bureaucrats. Sometimes it feels good, but only for a short time.

Twenty years ago, I experienced a significant decrease in income. I had no insurance, struggled to start my own business, and couldn't keep up with my bills. Eventually, I gained full employment and asked to see my credit report. On it were "charge-offs," where American Express and several companies, realizing I wasn't going to pay, just marked it as a charge-off. Those bad marks stay on the credit report for up to seven years and do not remove the obligation to repay them.

I made a list of charge-off marks against me, and unwilling to stiff somebody, I paid them off one by one as I could. Although it took work, contacting the companies, and settling each debt by working two jobs; I paid them all off. Eventually, my score went from the 500s to the 800s, where it has stayed to this day. Fair or not, the FICO credit score influences much of what you need to prosper in America until you have several million in cash.

When I worked in the prison system, I would talk to inmates about life "on the outside" and explain this credit scoring system to them. The FICO score is similar to the DA photo requirement. Most were unaware of it. I emphasized how important it was to their future, whether they, like me, resented it or not. They all took it to heart, as I doubt anyone had ever taken the time to teach them such things before.

So **keep your personnel file up to date**. In the civilian world, credit reports serve as their equivalent. Whether we like it or not!

Your credit score affects your life.

Chapter 26

Move Like You've Got a Purpose

I've saved this lesson for last, out of chronological order, involving once again CPT Phillips, in hopes it is one you will remember and because it is one I often repeat as a retiree in my comings and goings. I learned it in ROTC.

If you believe we teach people how to treat us, and that we define who we are by what we say "No" to, then we establish a reputation, good or bad, one way or another. Another factor contributing to our reputation is how we walk. That's right, walk, not just words, not just hairstyles, but also our gait. CPT Phillips counseled so frequently about walking that there is no one incident or event for me to share; instead, his constant mantra drives the point home: "Move like you've got a purpose!"

It is as valid a lesson for me as a senior citizen as it was in my twenties. It says something about the person. When you see a young teen meandering through the door of his workplace reporting for work, it creates the impression that "this fella doesn't want to be here, doesn't care about being here, and doesn't get paid enough to want to be here."

It's not rocket science. We've all seen it for ourselves. Consider the contrary: a young person going to work, moving quickly with solid steps, not dragging their feet, and moving as if they have a reason for doing what they are doing. We all would take that individual more seriously than the first example.

When I was placed under CPT Phillips' tutelage, I was nineteen. Most of my peers were already twenty, not old enough to buy beer in Missouri, and I hadn't been old enough to vote in a presidential election. We were kids on the way to shedding our teen habits. From this context, CPT Phillips would firmly state, "**Move like you've got a purpose!**" It didn't matter if we were walking to class or the dining hall; he impressed that refrain on us.

As my son was growing up, he would sometimes slouch a bit, drag his feet, as kids often do, and I would restate CPT Phillips' guidance. We might be walking from the grocery store back to the car, and I'd say it, even if it weren't necessary, just wanting him to hear it. Invariably, it would devolve into a race to the car to see who could touch it first, and it was a fun event for us.

This lesson is short, but it's one of the top ones to retain and to pass on to your children and grandchildren. When you walk with a purpose, people get out of your way, and they have a good impression of you. "There goes a man on a mission," or "That woman knows what she's doing!" and they'll take you seriously before they are ever introduced to you.

Thanks again, CPT Phillips!

Now we'll return to the chronology and look at how I chose to leave the US Army.

Chapter 27

End of Time in Service (ETS)

Seven years on active duty, two years in the Army Reserve as a captain, and I left as a major. The Army gave me a lot, but one thing they didn't give me beyond my paycheck was money. Not that I served for free; they paid me, and at the time, it was more than I'd ever had, even with the $800 a month take-home pay (see 1980 pay scale on next page). I was grateful! What I mean is that they didn't fund my education, and they didn't provide a 401(k) plan for me to roll over when I left. Once you're a captain, promotion to major is not automatic; it's competitive. You only get two chances to make major, and if you don't get promoted, you're forced out. The funny thing is, the Army gave captains who could not get promoted a separation bonus of $35,000 or more, which is about fifteen months' worth of pay!

Officer pay chart for under 2 years to 6 years of service.

Pay Grade	Years of Service				
	Under 2	Over 2	Over 3	Over 4	Over 6
O-10 See Note 2	3932.90	4081.50	4081.50	4081.50	4081.50
O-9	3494.40	3586.20	3662.40	3662.40	3662.40
O-8	3165.00	3259.80	3337.20	3337.20	3337.20
O-7	2629.80	2808.90	2808.90	2808.90	2934.60
O-6	1949.40	2142.00	2281.80	2281.80	2281.80
O-5	1559.10	1830.90	1957.20	1957.20	1957.20
O-4	1314.30	1599.90	1707.00	1707.00	1738.20
O-3	1221.30	1365.30	1459.50	1614.50	1692.00
O-2	1064.70	1163.10	1397.10	1444.20	1474.20
O-1	924.30	962.10	1163.10	1163.10	1163.10

See the irony? If you can't get promoted, you get a bonus. Get promoted, leave, receive another medal and a thank-you, but no cash. LOL. Gotta love it! It's partly why it's called "service." Compared to my civilian peers, I was seven years behind in retirement planning. That's okay. I wasn't sore about it; I found it more amusing than anything. I knew the deal and the rules when I signed up. I got to live in Germany again; the birth of my son cost me about $10 in medical bills. I had the opportunity to live and work in the nation's capital. I received tax-free housing subsidies (called Variable Housing Allowance, VHA), and I didn't have to buy a lot of suits and ties or worry about what I would wear the next morning. Beyond the money, these experiences I've shared with you clearly show that I gained a multitude of intangibles for which I am forever thankful.

Why did I get out? There are multiple reasons. While stationed at Davison Airfield, my unit held a change of command ceremony. We were getting a new "bird," Colonel—a West Pointer who had commanded another signal battalion at Coleman Barracks while I served in Charlie Company. Coincidence? Fate? Destiny? After that Friday's change of command ceremony, I drove home to our townhome in Burke, VA.

The lights were off, and no one greeted me. I walked into an empty house and read the note from my wife, which said, "Obviously Matthew and I are gone; we are still in the area; I will get in touch."

I faced a new commander and a major life reversal all within three hours. Now, that's not why I got out of the Army; I'm just revealing the context of my life then. Not long after, my tour at the airfield ended, I became the training officer at our headquarters at Fort McNair, where I endured the supervision of LTC Mann, who was, if anything, as particular an individual as I've ever met. He told us not to talk to him when we saw him in the hallway, beyond a simple hello, calling it being "shanghai'd." (Shanghai'd describes the practice of ship employees kidnapping men and forcing them into becoming sailors.) LTC Mann enjoyed playing word games, going from "happy" to "glad" and back again. He disallowed any correspondence leaving our unit that he had not personally approved. He loved "improving" everyone's writing skills, and he made his corrections with a green flair pen. I believe he enjoyed it, marking papers up in green, handing them back to us for rewriting, taking our visible frustration as his reward. We called his pen "the green weenie."

Luckily, he assigned Major Rob Lindsey, a West Pointer, to supervise me, but that only softened the inevitable conflict that was bound to happen.

One time, Major Lindsey and I were in Colonel Cargill's office, with birds on his shoulders, discussing an important matter.

He looked at me and said, "You know the 97th was a half-stepping outfit."

"Half-stepping" is an insult that describes the lazy and uncommitted. I responded strongly with, "That's Bullshit, Sir!" I then mentioned a field problem where we came to their rescue because his unit was unable to establish a radio link. At that point, Major Lindsey rushed me out of the office and stayed behind to chat with the colonel.

After finishing with Cargill, he found me, pulled me to the side, and said, "Look, Scott, I don't get it. I think you're a fine officer; you're intelligent, capable, and I've seen this type of thing before. It doesn't make sense, but for whatever reason, he's never going to have the opinion of you that I have."

I said, "Why? Our time in Germany is past; I should be judged for the present."

Major Lindsey replied, "You know, when I was in Vietnam, I saw people I knew who I thought were solid, well-trained, and shared the same values. But then I saw them do some of the strangest things I would have never expected. **Sometimes you just have to cut your losses.** Your best bet is to find another assignment before he can do damage to your career."

Fortunately, the Signal Officer in the 3rd US Infantry Regiment (The Old Guard) was leaving, which created a need for a new Signal Officer. I scheduled an appointment to meet with a LTC there and informed him of my desire to serve in that role. They valued my local experience and my previous service as the Signal Officer at The Army Aviation Brigade at Davison. I felt as though I had found a job, thus sparing myself from further misery with LTC Mann and Colonel Cargill.

I relished the idea of serving in the unit that guards the Tomb of the Unknown Soldier, performs funerals at Arlington, and, in emergencies, evacuates the President to safety. Soon thereafter, I told the colonel what I had done; he had to approve my departure, and I was certain he'd let me go. I don't remember Major Lindsey being in his office with me, but he must have been, as he wouldn't have wanted me alone with the colonel, for my benefit.

"The Old Guard, huh? Well, Captain, you're not going anywhere, you're staying right here."

I didn't pout, I didn't quibble, I didn't protest; I just said, 'Okay,' turned around, and walked out.

I remember the words of Uncle Lou, my father's brother, who made sergeant in the USMC within three years, telling me, "I would have stayed if I thought I could trust the people above me."

That still wasn't enough to make me leave the Army. Once, after staining my work with the "green weenie," I found myself back in LTC Mann's office. I accomplished a task in two days that typically would have taken thirty. He wanted me to do it the slow way. I said, "Sir, I think this is the best way to get it done, and it saves other units an annoyance."

He immediately got pissed off, clenched his fist, slammed it on the desktop, and yelled, "I DON'T WANT YOU TO THINK!"

I replied, "No problem, Sir, wouldn't have it any other way," and completed it his way. (It turned out I was right after all).

In another instance of "the green weenie" ruining my work, I frustratedly said to him, "Sir, I hate this style over substance crap."

He looked at me and replied, "You're in the wrong business." He was right.

During this time, I lost the child custody case, the judge approved my soon-to-be ex-wife's move to Dallas, and after they left, I received orders for a one-year assignment to Korea.

That's why I decided to leave. I didn't want to spend a year so far away from Matthew without seeing him. I turned down the orders and called my friend from the Signal Corps, Paul Krebs, now in Massachusetts, who had left the Army about a year before I did. Paul had a job with the phone company GTE in Needham and could help me get hired if I was interested. That's exactly what I did.

Know what's funny? Paul had been a Lieutenant in Germany under the battalion command of that same West Pointer, then Lieutenant Colonel Cargill.

Unfortunately, I outlasted Colonel Cargill in that unit, and his replacement was Colonel Fitz-Ens. I was already in the middle of out-processing, and I'm sorry I didn't get to stay and serve under him. Unlike the outgoing commander, Colonel Fitz-Ens expressed that he wasn't afraid of not becoming a General Officer; he was comfortable speaking directly to subordinates and cared more about accurate information than perceptions. He was my kind of officer. Both commanders retired as Colonels, and Colonel Fitz-Ens went on to publish the book *Why a Soldier?*

I moved to Boston. In Massachusetts, I tried to get into the Army Reserve. Some of my coworkers were in the 76th Infantry Division, a training division, in Providence, RI. I met with them and received a notice stating they had plenty of captains and my service was not needed. I accepted that, then started growing my hair out and looking less military. I enjoyed that for a while until Saddam Hussein occupied Kuwait. A week later, I received orders assigning me to the 76th with a reporting date the following month.

"Needs of the Service." HA!

I enrolled in the two-year correspondence course version of Command and General Staff College as required, left GTE, and became a registered representative with Edward Jones. The job demanded a significant amount of time, and being recently married with a blended family, I had too many obligations.

As if Joseph Heller wrote my Army career, I received a letter from Major Fogerty at the 76th. I was no longer living in New England, but I still occupied a CPT slot, which meant some lieutenant in Rhode Island could not get promoted. "Congratulations," he wrote, "the Army has deigned to make you a Major, badda-boom, badda-bing, there are no open slots in the 76th for Majors and you are out of the unit, free to go find a slot elsewhere." I got promoted to major without that DA photo, but I was removed from the unit in Rhode Island. Army wins!

And that's how my military career ended.

Lessons here? Yeah, there are jerks everywhere. Uncle Lou (USMC), who retired as an executive at Kodak, once advised me that **success at work hinges significantly on choosing your boss wisely**. It's true, and like Major Lindsey told me, sometimes you have to cut your losses and go. I hope that if you're going through tough times with a supervisor, you remember this, and I hope even more that you aren't one of those supervisors to be avoided.

Chapter 28

Epilogue

To me, the best part of the Army now is the memories. Running in formation—both strenuous and motivating. Coming to attention in formation and hearing just one click of boots, CPT Phillips telling us to "get down and start knocking 'em out!" (his call for push-ups), and "Move like you've got a purpose" all bring moments of personal joy. Standing at the head of a convoy as all the two-and-a-half-ton diesels fire up, ready to cross the line of departure just after sunrise? It's exhilarating, the start of an adventure! Experiencing a hot breakfast outside on a cold morning, mail call, and heating a can of C-rations on a generator muffler—I cherish those memories.

But the Army is not the Boy Scouts. Soldiers get killed, and some do the killing. The Army, the military, carries a greater risk of physical trauma than many occupations, but it does not have a monopoly on this issue. Trauma affects everyone and can be hidden inside a person, not necessarily visible through physical observation. I'm not a licensed therapist; I passed Psychology 101 as an undergraduate, but that's it, so I can't diagnose, but I can share my experiences, and I want to offer you and the Army a recommendation.

Firstly, I disavow the notion that one person's suffering is worse than another's. You don't know. You can guess. You can even make a rational guess. Most of the time, such comparisons are secretly intended to comfort the person doing the comparing.

"You watched your dog get run over; at least it wasn't a child." That's true, but what's the purpose of saying such a thing?

The pet owner is not going to say: "You're right about that, I guess I'll be happy now."

Doesn't that seem silly? The person said it for their benefit, not the grieving person's. Both events are traumatic. We've all experienced trauma. Yes, you, too. I know I have. None of us has a golden dome protecting us from it, and for many people, the trauma comes from members of their own family.

Psychologists have different definitions of trauma. While this isn't my main topic, I encourage you to explore and read various interpretations. I don't intend to pretend I can provide a definitive take on Post Traumatic Stress Disorder (PTSD) either, but I can share some insights. Trauma occurs, and behavior is a consequence. One quote in particular that resonated with me is: "When you understand the trauma, the behavior makes sense." A word of caution: "understanding" does not imply acceptance. Consider this scenario: an engaged woman whose father died young and whose mother was likely a sociopath, and often discussed abandoning her at orphanages, has a fiancé now who mentions he's looking for a job 300 miles away. She reacts wildly, unable to discuss it calmly. That's trauma. This doesn't mean she is excused from other behaviors or that she is exempt from the requirement to speak maturely about the job prospect and how they would manage such a transition in their life. However, it does make her response understandable. It makes sense that she reacts this way, but it should not be considered acceptable behavior.

The Army, nay, the entire world, has walking wounded of this sort. Everyone suffers post-traumatic stress; it's natural. We're designed that way. Viktor Frankl told us in his book *Man's Search for Meaning* that an abnormal reaction to an abnormal situation is normal behavior. It's only a disorder when the behavior interrupts function, recurrently, over time. That's when it becomes a disorder.

My story: In 1984, we had an aircraft go down, killing all four on board, and I had to listen to the tapes, the final conversations and last words of the pilots to my controller, over and over. In 1993, my bride was killed six days before our first wedding anniversary, hit by a train on her way to work one Monday morning in July. To put it mildly, I was heartbroken, crushed, and demoralized. In 2004, a little Iraqi girl, maybe four years old, whom I used to see regularly through the other side of the perimeter fence, was run over by an American veteran turned truck driver. I listened to his lamenting for hours as he sat outside processing what the hell happened. I had been talking with a therapist and thought I was doing fine. I was. I was working, paying my bills, visiting my son, and maintaining relationships (though they were turbulent). One time, I was at a stoplight waiting to turn left, and a guy acted like he wasn't going to stop while I had the green arrow. I made the turn, stopped in the middle of the road, blocking traffic, and immediately put the vehicle in Park. I jumped out of my car and ran towards his car to start a fistfight because of how I perceived his infraction. Luckily, he kept driving, and no words were exchanged.

I told the therapist, Donna, this story, and I said, "I don't know what's going on, but something's wrong." She referred me to a colleague trained in a therapy called EMDR (Eye Movement Desensitization and Reprocessing). It's intended for treating trauma (which means all of us). We made an appointment, and Donna wanted to go as an observer, and I consented. The entire experience lasted approximately fifty minutes. At first, I thought, *'This is goofy; I'm not staying.'* But I did. It was the most emotionally intense thing I've ever done. I bawled my eyes out.

Afterwards, on my way home, it felt like a burden had been lifted; I hadn't felt that good in years! I was happy again. EMDR is an impressive technique, and it generally only requires a few sessions. As a result, the therapist, Donna, became licensed in EMDR herself and includes it as part of her practice (assuming she has not since retired). This is my recommendation to the Army and you, my friend: EMDR.

Without minimizing the significance of these events, trauma isn't always so dramatic. Its impact however is just as severe. A divorce, a parent calling you a moron who'll never amount to anything, and a spouse cheating on you are all intensely traumatic.

We have multitudes of ex-military personnel who have returned with post-traumatic stress. The risk of a military career increases the probability of some occupational trauma. My experience forces me to conclude that EMDR can help thousands of soldiers and prevent the trauma from becoming a disorder. It would be awesome to urge the VA

(Veterans Affairs) and our Congress to include EMDR as a primary treatment plan for our veterans and active-duty members. However, I am less concerned with starting a campaign than I am with you and your loved ones who live with trauma. Many who deal with trauma end up hurting themselves, developing addiction, isolating themselves, experiencing anger, and even violence. It is not an inaccurate description that "hurting people, hurt people." EMDR offers an increased probability of trauma no longer predicting behavior.

I learned from the US Army, and now I hope they learn from me.

As for me? I've never remarried, came close several times, and am now living on a pension and social security, in a home too big for me. I still wrestle with the devils of isolation and overeating, but I know that God cannot steer a ship that's not moving. So, I exercise, love renting places in Key West or Europe, see my son and sister, play guitar, and listen to my son play (he's much better, by the way!). I remain grateful for the Army that taught me to move with purpose and how to survive well in life!

References

Covey, Stephen R. 1989. *The 7 Habits of Highly Effective People*. New York: Simon & Schuster.

Compton, Arthur Holly. 1956. *Atomic Quest: A Personal Narrative*. New York: Oxford University Press. Quoted in Doug Long.

"General Marshall's Views on the Atomic Bomb." Accessed August 26, 2025. http://www.doug-long.com/marshall.htm.

www.ingramcontent.com/pod-product-compliance
Lightning Source LLC
Chambersburg PA
CBHW070920130626
46555CB00001B/212